HUMAN RIGHTS

DAVID OWEN

HUMAN RIGHTS

W · W · NORTON & COMPANY

New York   London

Library of Congress Cataloging in Publication Data

Owen, David, 1938–
  Human rights.

  Includes index.
  1. Civil rights. I. Title.
JC571.094 1978   323.4   78–13668
ISBN 0–393–01186–0

1 2 3 4 5 6 7 8 9 0

Contents

I

Human Rights in Britain

Human rights have been at the centre of the development of British politics ever since Magna Carta—upheld by individuals, fought for by Cromwell, championed by the trade unions, highlighted by the suffragettes and influenced by the churches. The debate on human rights is often depicted as an issue between countries but it is primarily an issue within countries. The espousal of human rights involves a commitment to values; and a readiness to identify and live up to those values at home before, as individuals or as a state, we can expect to carry conviction abroad.

What are the values, and beliefs, of our own society? Even to pose the question is to challenge those who look with suspicion on any attempt to invoke morality, ethics, principles and values in a political context. There is a view—particularly prevalent amongst political commentators—which castigates any attempt to look beyond practical pragmatic policies, depicting it as preaching, moralising and do-gooding. In fact it is often those same commentators who delight in identifying politicians as self-seeking, ambitious, cynical and power-hungry. It was the ancient Greeks who saw politics as a noble profession involved in the very essence of living and who proclaimed that a person bored with politics was bored with life. To divorce the values of society from the politics of society is a grave error and risks the cheapening of both and the weakening of society itself. Yet values are personal to individuals; though they have universal application they cannot be separated from one's own individual philosophy and social objectives. We must identify our own values and those of the society we wish to live in before relating them to a policy for human rights either at home or abroad.

I am sometimes criticised for talking too much about moral values, for trying to draw attention to the latent altruism that I believe exists within most individuals and which is often not fully tapped. I do not believe that the politician or the public man in whatever walk of life can ignore morality and ethics. I do not believe that a country can operate in the world without trying to project abroad its own ethical values, its own moral principles. Once you say that, however, you become a victim for those people to whom consistency is itself an absolute value, to whom any deviation from principle is somehow seen as weakness, and for those who want to elevate to an unnatural level an inflexible and rigid hierarchy of values.

When I began to speak out for human rights and argued that a concern for human rights should permeate our whole foreign policy, I warned that there was a price to pay, and that the price was a little inconsistency from time to time. If I had to make that comment again, I would no longer say a *little* inconsistency, I would say a *very great deal* of inconsistency. Yet because those inconsistencies are probed and exposed publicly and often turned against the person who wishes to try to promote a sense of values, there is a danger that people will cease to proclaim principles and values; because they cannot be consistent and cannot always justify every stance against previously stated or previously believed principles, they will cease to inject this particular issue into public life at all. And because the politician's compromises are very obvious, can be seen by everyone, can be dissected, editorialised upon and scathingly attacked, there has been a tendency to elevate, possibly to an unrealistic height, the attraction of the man in public life who is the man of principle, the man of consistency, the man of unbending views.

I tend to believe, perhaps because I am a doctor and as such a behavioural scientist, that human nature and its values, though profound and even sacred to the individual, are so personal and so unique that there are not, nor can there be, absolute in values. I have been profoundly influenced by the writings of Sir Isaiah Berlin and his most recent book, *Russian Thinkers* (Hogarth Press, 1978). While there are common themes to life, and thankfully a great deal of agreement

2

about values in society, there is in my view an inevitable conflict of values—and what is more, an inevitable conflict on the interpretation of values. This conflict is to me both natural and right and makes human behaviour unique, satisfying and full of variety In my view there is bound to be a moral conflict. We accept and operate within rules of society built up over centuries because we know ourselves, because we know that without rules, without conventions, we would break down into individual units, each pulling in our own direction, and we accept those rules as part of the cement of our society.

I am not, as I have made clear, a believer in a utopian society. I am not one who thinks that there is a single vision, who seeks order in society when I believe that though order is necessary it can never be perfect. I do not seek certainty or conformity because I do not believe that the difficult choices in life allow one to be perfectly consistent. I am prepared to face and indeed to praise the agony of choice that exists in society for each and every one of us. I do not crave the certainty of order. I am not prepared to forgo the independent spirit. I do not want to replace a certain individuality and variety with precision and conformity. I do not see compromise as weakness. I see it instead as strength.

The British tradition of democratic socialism, both drawing on and promoting the value of altruism, is the one with which I identify and from which I derive inspiration. British socialism has never been dogmatic or prescriptive. Its strength has lain in its practical, non-doctrinal attack on poverty and inequality, and in the variety of political traditions from which it has evolved—fabianism and co-operativism, guild socialism and utopianism, marxism, pacifism and Christian commitment. There have always been contradictions between the various strands which make up British socialism—between participation and paternalism, between collectivist and libertarian instincts and between statism and the anarchic tradition of de-centralised power. The mix produces a political alliance which is both irascible and indefinable. Regrettably socialism sometimes appears to be a doctrine motivated by envy but, uniquely among political movements, it can claim that in its practical decisions and actions it has been motivated at times by sheer love. Whatever the disagreements over policy, there has been over the years a striking degree of unanimity on the basic values underlying the individual socialist commitment. Yet today that unanimity over values is not as apparent as it has been in the past, if for no other reason than that we have grown reluctant to discuss the values of socialism.

Cynicism dominates our media: we are often afraid to talk about fundamentals for fear of being mocked. Yet socialism depends more than any other political philosophy on the latent altruism within us all. If socialists fail to tap, ignite, cherish and foster altruism they will never enlist sufficient support for their policies. Socialism is not dedicated to the values of the market place, where *what does it cost?* and *what is it worth?* predominate. The critics of socialism would dearly like to cast it as the stifler of individualism, the breeder of bureaucracies, fanatically elevating the power of the state in an intrusive and unfeeling manner. It is the form, the control and the responsiveness of the administration which determines whether it is a bureaucracy. An administrator is not synonymous with a bureaucrat. While there always were bureaucrats and statists among British socialists, British socialism as such has never been committed to these attitudes. Community co-operation, participation, workers' democracy, de-centralised decision-making, the virtue of the small unit—these, on the other hand, have always been valued in British socialism, yet until recently they seem to have been less influential and the socialist philosophy and appeal correspondingly weakened.

At last we are moving away from ever-increasing centralisation. The enacting of legislation for Scottish devolution is a welcome return to a historic commitment. In criticising the 1973 local government reforms we are searching for ways of bringing closer to the people some of the decision-making powers which were then placed in the hands of large and impersonal structures.

The identification of the Labour Party as a party of bureaucratic collectivism and state power is, in part, a consequence of its becoming a party of government. Committed to public ownership, Labour Ministers have had to take whole industries automatically into *state* ownership, until the formation of the

4

National Enterprise Board. We had not until recently sought to devise ways and means of ensuring worker and public participation, concentrating instead on ownership at the expense of accountability. State-orientated nationalisation was understandable as a post-war policy. We have, however, paid a heavy price for the sterile public ownership arguments of the 1950s. Few now question that the lesson of the experience of the 1960s and 1970s is that old-style state ownership is not sustainable as a coherent socialist answer to the industrial and economic problems of the 1980s. We have begun to rethink our attitudes.

If we look back to the late 1940s, we see a Labour Government concerned, essentially, with enacting legislation and implementing policies brought out and argued through in the 1920s and 1930s. Planning, the welfare state, full employment, and public ownership of several key industries were long-term socialist policies which the Attlee Government put into effect. They followed years of socialist discussion against a background of mass unemployment, depression, fascism and war. Important changes in the lifestyle of the mass of the population followed. Car-ownership became general and the drift from the inner city to affluent suburbs accelerated. Pre-war socialist talk of 'wage-slavery' lost credibility, a more hedonistic public mood was engendered. Yet even so, in 1951 the Labour Government only just lost power. It still stood for identifiable values and it actually polled the largest vote ever given to any single party in our history.

The material prosperity of the 1950s and the apparently ever-rising living standards of the population led many to conclude that the bad old days had gone for ever, and with them the relevance of socialist values. The Conservatives, elected with increasing majorities in 1955 and 1959, seemed in tune with the national mood. Yet while Mr Macmillan told the country, 'You've never had it so good,' the gap between private affluence and public squalor became more apparent and led to the socialist counter-demand for higher public expenditure. The new socialist wisdom was that the conflict between public expenditure and private consumption would be solved painlessly, without the need for choosing, by economic growth. Full employment and rapid growth in the economy would, it was argued, ensure that socialists could avoid unpleasant choices over redistribution simply by ensuring that the additional resources coming from economic growth were fairly distributed. For the Labour Party, which seemed at the beginning of the 1960s to be doomed to eternal opposition, and was caught up in the polemics between the rival claims of revisionism and fundamentalism, the elixir of economic growth became the rallying point. The underlying issues were fudged by generating a feeling that technique was everything and that the discoveries of science and technology would somehow solve political problems. It epitomised an attitude which impregnated our national life. It led to the belief that there were simple technical solutions to complex problems and with it came the trivialisation of political values and political debate.

The 1970s are hard to assess. They are still with us. But when history is written, it is highly probable that the dominant theme will be seen to have been the world economic recession. Management of the economy has been the central issue. Out of the trauma of confrontation in the early 1970s there developed a philosophy of containment, back to work and slow, painful readjustment to reality after the shock of a five-fold increase in oil prices. The deep-seated world economic recession continued but a Labour Government deploying the arts of government replaced the technical-managerial, stainless-steel attitudes of the previous Conservative administration. Whereas in 1974 the question posed was, 'Is Britain governable?', the question at the next election will be, 'How should Britain be governed?' This is in itself a formidable achievement and represents a transformation of public attitudes. It has been a painful period of readjustment but the basic stability of British society has reasserted itself.

In the wake of the complacency of the 1950s and the slick technocratic confidence of the 1960s, the late 1970s seem to usher in an era of realism. This realism is born of disillusionment and cynicism. It has produced, however, a reawakening of interest in political values, especially at the extremes of politics, and regrettably to date more on the right than on the left.

It is illustrated at its most crass level by the contrasting extremisms of the Socialist Workers' Party and the National

Front. The centre, always somewhat sceptical about ideology, has produced little new thinking but also and more importantly has weakened its own appeal through its neglect of, and reluctance to declare its belief in, political values. The philosophical left and the philosophical right have gained ground and converts.

The rise of the philosophical right is one of the most noticeable features of the British political scene in the last few years. In rejecting altogether Butskellism and Heathian managerialism, and lacking an aristocracy, some Conservatives have sought to reassert what they see as traditional conservative values — values such as thrift, self-reliance and personal initiative. Groups centred around such ventures as the publication of the Black Paper have proselytised the values of elitism and though they have rightly championed standards they have come close to advocating exclusivity in education. Private health schemes have been extolled; the National Health Service has been subjected to insidious and totally unjustified criticism by those who wish to undermine its essentially ethical basis. The manifestations of privilege have been portrayed as the rewards of initiative and the failures of state provision have been represented as the inevitable consequence of 'socialist' bureaucracy. The National Association for Freedom campaigns for the freedom of the 'little man' against — as it sees it — the dictatorial powers of the big battalions of the trade unions and the abuses of doctrinaire politicians. Instead of counter-attacking with a studied socialist critique of a conservatively organised society, the left has appeared philosophically exhausted and we have seen recently the growth of a new right-wing onslaught against what is represented as 'socialist' Britain.

Socialists ignore this criticism at their peril, for this view has considerable credibility to those in our society who appear to be losing power. This is not just the 'middle class'; it can be the skilled craftsman seeing differentials eroded and jealous of the power of the big public service or general trade unions; or it can be the housewife on a council estate frustrated and eager to listen to anything which offers a prospect of change and who wants better services and lower taxes and does not sense the inconsistency of those who promise both.

7

The new right is succeeding very skilfully in discrediting the ideals of socialism by pointing to the failures of bureaucratic or statist policies—policies which often have been actually introduced and certainly maintained by Conservative Governments and which are not in themselves socialist at all. Many aspects of the new right's philosophy which socialists would strongly oppose—their support for elitism, their exploitation of racial tensions within Britain, their apologia for economic inequality, their attitude towards those who through inadequacy of temperament, education or upbringing find difficulty in coping with life—obscure many valid points about what is wrong with the society socialists appear to favour in this country. The slogan *More means Worse* aphorises values which are an anathema to socialists, but the criticism, for example, of large schools under the slogan *Big means Bad* is not merely fashionable rightist dogma but fair criticism.

Socialists are at last giving long overdue attention to the content of education, not merely to its structure. It is increasingly recognised that the quality of care in the Health and Social Services has been neglected in the pursuit of quantity. The left is far less dismissive now than in the past about the motivation of the voluntary movement and has become involved with it. It is important, welcome and true to its traditions that a Labour Government has been sponsoring 'Good Neighbour Campaigns' and giving increased financial support to voluntary bodies such as MIND, NACRO, CHAR and CARE. Yet if the Labour movement ignores its basic values, and allows itself to be represented, albeit often unfairly, as the party of bureaucracy and the big battalions, as a party which confuses equality with sameness and democratic ownership and accountability with statism, an ideological new right will increasingly grow up which will use the failures of socialism in power to discredit socialist values and objectives in theory.

Some of the energies, idealism and commitment of the traditional centre socialist are already finding their outlet beyond the framework of conventional politics. In the last ten years or so pressure groups have grown up—like the Disablement Income Group, the Child Poverty Action Group, Shelter, Oxfam and the Friends of the Earth—attracting people who

tend to see a virtue in being apolitical and in not being be-
holden or unduly committed to any one political party. Rather
than joining a political party, they involve themselves in pressure groups dealing with specific areas of policy, or throw their
energies into protests over local issues like the route of a
motorway or the site of a new airport. In the United States and
in Western Europe this trend is discernible too; in France groups
have contested elections under the banner of 'Ecologism' and
have done remarkably well. Here again the Labour Government is sensing the mood. The decision to hold a public enquiry
into the plans for a nuclear thermal reactor reprocessing plant
at Windscale, and the subsequent public and Parliamentary
debate, showed the Government to be sensitive to the public
mood. Even if the environmentalists did not agree with the
final verdict, the measured way in which it was reached represented a major development in democratic decision-making.

Radical thinking is not dead in Britain. The wish to change
society remains—particularly amongst the young—but it has
been nearly strangled by committees: ideas and problems are
endlessly referred for committee decision-making where, under
the guise of democratic involvement, the spirit of challenge,
initiative and even risk is deadened and dulled. Ideas are
stifled by the 'bureaucratic embrace' of Whitehall in central
government or Town Hall in local government. The 'dogmatic
embrace'—of political parties clinging to outmoded attitudes—
is another factor in curbing change in British society.

Much of current political language is ritually divisive and so
polarised that it strikes very few sparks and fails to stimulate
commitment in the young. Much of the current political debate
is outdated, artificial and frequently irrelevant. The language
is rarely inspiring and though inevitably technical infrequently
draws on underlying values.

The role of values is to inspire, to guide, to appeal to the
altruistic element in everyone. If socialism is associated in
people's minds with dictatorial or insensitive bureaucratic
control, with large impersonal institutions and the rule of
cliques, not only does it not deserve to succeed politically bu it
is the antithesis of socialist values. The strength of socialist
values, their power to call forth the best in men, is what dif-

9

ferentiates the Labour Party from its opponents. As one writer has put it: while Conservatives believe in 'original sin', and believe that institutions should be designed to curb human instincts, the socialist sees the institutions as the bad influence, distorting and deforming the essential goodness of man.

In his study of the relationship between human blood and social policy, *The Gift Relationship* (Allen and Unwin, 1971), Richard Titmuss says:

> No money values can be attached to the presence or absence of a spirit of altruism in a society. Altruism in giving to a stranger ... may touch every aspect of life and affect the whole fabric of value. Its role in satisfying the biological need to help — particularly in modern societies — is another immeasurable element.

Titmuss also notes the crucial omission in Marx's critique of capitalism of any formulation of a morality for a socialist society. He also emphasises Marx's crude utilitarianism.

The essential value of socialism is altruism. The eradication of inequalities and the striving for a more egalitarian society are aims inspired by that value. The dilemma comes with the word equality, easy to espouse, yet impossible wholly to fulfil. Contrasting inequalities — in lifestyles, skills and other attributes — not only exist but are actively maintained by all Governments of the left, whether communist or social democrat. The system of differential rewards is maintained unchallenged. This inconsistency between rhetoric and action demands a more open discussion of equality if it is to carry conviction as part of a socialist philosophy. The concept of equality has been devalued by its obvious unobtainability and by its imperfect implementation. It can easily take on a drab, mechanistic connotation. Some writers have tried to substitute other words — 'fairness', 'justice'. Perhaps 'equity' is the most accurate word to describe the actuality rather than the objective of equality. Socialists are concerned with differences in class, status and power. All three remain very unevenly distributed in our society. Yet the socialist who identifies himself with an egalitarian philosophy soon finds a conflict between the espousal of equality and the living of a life of inequality whether in terms of class, status or power. This contrast between one's actual lifestyle and one's theoretical lifestyle is both the contradiction and the inspiration of socialism. The same conflict exists between the values of liberty and of equality. That conflict is inevitable; the response to it is not. We can either be inspired by the contradiction to strive both to reduce inequalities and to enlarge individual liberty or we can so adjust ourselves and our attitudes that the inequalities remain, liberty is restricted and the basis of socialism is eroded.

Social engineering or manipulation is not of itself an answer. Attitudinal change is crucial. We also need to look long and hard at class divisions in the fields of industry, education and housing in order to encourage social desegregation. We need to look at school catchment areas and at zoning policies in housing. We are now tackling as a matter of extreme urgency the growing division between prosperous, well-provided-for suburbs where white families live, and the broken down, inner city areas where the poor, the deprived, the single-parent families, the old, and the blacks are concentrated. We need to encourage debate and knowledge of these contrasts and deprivations within our society.

Democracy in Britain is so deep-rooted that we barely need to emphasise its role as a fundamental value. It clearly divides the left and in particular the small British Communist Party from the Labour Party. Democratic socialism manifests itself in different forms in different countries but respect for the ballot-box reflects an underlying respect for the views of others. Democracy is not limited to national and local elections. It is essentially about participation and control and one of its immediate developments is its application to workers' participation and control, which is a noble ideal and a basic aim of socialism. Yet workers' control has been abused and devalued in the hands of its enemies and has sometimes been cheapened even by its advocates. Typically it has been identified by some as an extension of collectivism. There is now a strong belief that it can only be effectively developed if prescribed in legislative form. Legislation will be necessary, but there are grave dangers in prescribing a rigid centralised format. The real need is for a legislative pattern which will foster its development but will allow variety, flexibility and experiment and will be able to match the demands of different industries and different groups of people.

Socialism is participation, responsibility and democracy. The guild socialists saw this fifty and sixty years ago; the points they were making are more relevant than ever today. S. T. Glass, in his useful monograph on guild socialism, *The Responsible Society* (Longman, 1966), has summarised the guild socialist argument:

> Under the existing industrial system the worker was treated not as a human being entitled to be considered as a partner in the enterprise, but as a living tool ... standing to his employer in just the same relation as the machine he minds stands to himself.
>
> The conventional kind of public ownership that would replace the capitalist by the bureaucrat did not change this condition.
>
> Such a passive role in employment was contrary to a proper conception of human purpose and dignity, and to the desire for self-expression and self-government that men possessed.
>
> Industrial autocracy bore particularly heavily upon its subjects because work played a central part in daily life. The denial to the working class of self-government in those aspects of the community's affairs that touched them most closely, and which were most intelligible to them, had the effect of stifling both interest and capacity to play a part in public life. The working class, a majority of the people, therefore played a passive role in politics.

Guild socialism was at bottom a plea for a more active democracy. An active democracy necessitates information. The inequality of information between shop floor and management is one of the major causes of attitudinal gaps. To bridge these gaps, to make participation real, there has to be equality of information and education on how to interpret such information.

Participation is a two-way process, as is democracy itself. Its basis is a regard for others' views, the fostering of a feeling of partnership or co-operation. Democracy establishes rights and responsibilities for the individual within a community.

A political philosophy that looks only at individuals or institutions and ignores the role of families will soon run into difficulties. Family life remains the linchpin of our society. It is a manifestation of collectivism in miniature, and should be buttressed and sustained as part of a family policy. Housing design, pre-school education, marriage guidance, leisure activities, adult education; these are not fringe issues but essential elements of a coherent socialist philosophy for family life. We ignore these issues at our peril. They matter. They are relevant to day-to-day life. One of the most potent threats to family life and indeed to the stability of society generally is boredom and frustration. The demoralisation that stems from the inability to provide sufficient jobs can hardly be exaggerated. Employment policies impact on many of the underlying problems of society—on delinquency, crime and violence. Jobs do not of themselves solve these problems, but their absence contributes to dissatisfaction and despair.

There are dangers in concentrating on rights when elaborating a political philosophy which spells out our duties as well as our rights. Human rights are a concept which cannot be proclaimed with any conviction merely by defining what rights an individual can claim from society. The individual must also contribute to that society; rights and duties go together.

Socialism is in many ways not as instinctive a philosophy as conservatism. Interdependence is not as well-established in most people's day-to-day lifestyle as independence and self-reliance. Community living is a reality, but the idea that 'an Englishman's home is his castle' is still a dominant reflex. Socialism needs to be argued for, explained and championed. Logically it is inevitable; instinctively many defy its logic. We have to battle for people's minds before we can be sure that their values will coincide with ours.

Socialism means nurturing the instinct to help one's neighbour to live as part of a community, it means answering basic human wishes to influence their destiny. Socialism means enlarging and nurturing the altruistic element in us all. The espousal of human rights is a radical policy, a natural policy for socialists to champion. It goes to the roots of our society and yet, to carry conviction, needs to stem not from empty rhetoric but from actually achieved and established rights across a whole range of human activity within our own society.

2

Human Rights Abroad

From the beginning of the decade developments in international affairs have helped to sharpen public concern in many different countries and continents about the condition of human rights worldwide. Since 1972 the Conference on Security and Co-operation in Europe process has placed human rights firmly on the agenda of East-West relations. There have been appalling violations of human rights in a number of countries of which Chile, Uganda, Cambodia and Ethiopia are the best known, but are far from being the only ones. Despite almost ceaseless political and diplomatic effort year in, year out, the Middle East problem appears to be as intractable as ever. Apartheid in South Africa and the continuing denial of self-determination and democratic freedoms to the peoples of Southern Africa underline the extent to which these problems are problems of elementary human rights. The establishment of a dialogue between the advanced industrialised nations and those of the developing world reminds us that economic deprivation, and the disease and malnutrition which go with it, are an equally intolerable abuse of human dignity.

All these things have raised the profile of human rights in international affairs and have compelled those who formulate foreign policy—at least in those democratic countries where public concern cannot be ignored by Governments—to give a higher priority than ever before to human rights.

This has been a sufficiently rapid, even dramatic, develop-ment to create the impression for some that peoples and Governments have only recently stumbled on the importance of human rights. The Governments of the Soviet Union and the other communist countries of Eastern Europe, for example, profess to see the West's concern for human rights as simply an opportunist and ephemeral twist in the ideological struggle, a struggle which detente has sharpened, not softened. This ignores the fact that the liberty of the individual and his relationship to the state have been issues fundamental to the development over the centuries of European philosophy and political theory; and that as East and West move further away from the open hostility of the Cold War, when simple survival was all that mattered, towards the more civilised relationship which detente is intended to promote, these issues must increasingly come to the fore. The present debate, conducted both internationally and within our separate societies, about the nature of human rights and how they can be safeguarded and extended is in direct line of descent from the first questioning of the moral certainties of mediaeval man which marked the beginning of modern times and which itself drew on an earlier classical tradition.

The belief, for instance, that certain rights are inalienable, guaranteeing the integrity of the person and the right to life itself, is central to humanitarian and democratic values today. But the same belief underpinned England's Bill of Rights in 1689, the American Declaration of Independence in 1776, and the French Declaration of the Rights of Man in 1789. All these constitutional landmarks drew their intellectual inspiration from a great body of seventeenth- and eighteenth-century thinkers such as Locke in England and the Rationalists in France; and all led to the further proposition—again crucial to democratic society today—that man's inalienable rights can only be guaranteed in a society in which political and civil liberties flourish—freedom of thought, expression, association, movement and participation in the democratic process. In Britain in the nineteenth century this proposition was further refined by thinkers such as Mill and Bentham and throughout the West found its practical expression in the gradual spread of democratic forms of government.

Economic and social rights, which deservedly receive so much attention today and which the Western democracies are sometimes accused of neglecting, have also for long been in the mainstream of our societies' development. The second Declaration of the Rights of Man in 1793 provided for the right to education, while the development over more than a century of trade union rights, democratic socialism and a whole complex of social legislation, on which what is sometimes known as the welfare state rests, testifies to the crucial importance of this category of rights in Western democratic life.

There is nothing novel or opportunist about the priority which member countries of the Council of Europe and other democracies today attach to human rights: it is, as it has been for centuries, an evolving concern of our peoples and of our Governments. But what is relatively new is the growing recognition, not just in the Western democracies but worldwide, that the abuse of human rights is the legitimate subject of international concern; and that the enforcement of human rights can no longer be left to national Governments alone. The basic premise of fundamental and internationally agreed documents such as the United Nations Charter, the Universal Declaration of Human Rights, the International Covenants of the United Nations, the European Convention of Human Rights essentially is that human rights stand on values which are the property of all men and which transcend national frontiers. Even here the break with the past is not total. In the nineteenth century the struggle between absolutism and liberalism in Europe, and the fate of the Spanish colonies in Latin America, aroused sufficient public sympathy in Britain for what were considered to be oppressed nationalities to influence the course of British foreign policy. The so-called Bulgarian Atrocities of 1876 provoked indignation in Europe and had a serious impact on the approach of the international community to the Balkan question.

Today, the main task of those of us who are trying coherently and consistently to integrate human rights considerations into the conduct of foreign policy is to devise the means by which respect for human rights can be more effectively guaranteed and enforced. Lord Acton may have been right in believing the Declaration of the Rights of Man to be more powerful than all Napoleon's armies but the power of moral example is seldom enough, at least where human rights are concerned.

The British Government tries to promote greater respect for human rights in its bilateral relations with countries where the situation gives cause for concern. We shall go on trying. But this is not an ideal or a sufficient way of going about things, requiring as it does a balance between the need for a consistent moral position, on the one hand, and, on the other, a hard-headed but necessary calculation of national interest, of the likely effectiveness or otherwise of any action which we may take and of the strength of public feeling at home. Different countries and different circumstances will require different measures and the Government will frequently be open to the charge of inconsistency. As one Foreign Secretary, George Canning, told the House of Commons in 1821, 'The price at which political liberty is to be valued, and the cost at which it is to be obtained, constitute the nicest balance.'

The basic British respect for the rule of law, individual liberty, fairness and democratic debate has had its influence worldwide through the Empire, Dominions, Colonies and Commonwealth. The debate continues within Britain but it is inevitable that, having ourselves made great progress towards extending human rights, we should wish to project that respect for human rights into all the countries of the world. The politics of human rights and the diplomacy of human rights are central to the development of British foreign policy. To understand how Britain can influence the international debate, we must first analyse our own foreign policy.

We are an island race, part of Europe, but with the Atlantic breaking against our coast. An accident of history brought the industrial revolution to Britain before any other European country. This, coupled with British sea power, gave us the wherewithal to trade and invest in almost every corner of the globe. Today, we are members of the European Community and our future lies with Europe. But the scale of our international interests is not such that we could withdraw from them even if we wished to do so. It is not a British instinct to seek to restrict our horizons and to think and act as if in a continental cocoon. The maritime influence is strong within us.

Yet Britain today has little yearning for past imperial glories. Over the past ten years we have become more realistic about our influence in the world. It is now time to stop selling ourselves short and to end our present mood of introspection and self-denigration. We need more self-confidence, more national buoyancy. We are in danger of exaggerating our weaknesses and of underplaying our potential. We have considerable strengths.

We hold a leading position in the European Community. It is not just one of the wealthiest and potentially most economically powerful groups in the world. The aspirations of the member states go beyond immediate national concerns. They are in principle and in practice prepared to forgo national advantage in return for longer-term Community advantage.

We are a country which is unusually dependent on foreign trade, with overseas investments second only to those of the United States. We remain the financial centre of the world. As a result, we have to be actively involved in the major international economic institutions—the OECD, the IMF and the GATT.

We are a vital element in the Atlantic Alliance and the only European member state of NATO which contributes to the strategic, tactical-nuclear and conventional forces of the Organisation. We have a continuing responsibility for Berlin, the exercise of which is vital to the stability of Europe. We are a permanent member of the UN Security Council. We are a member of the Commonwealth, which gives us a unique insight into the preoccupations and interests of thirty-five independent countries, covering a broad cross-section and a quarter of the world's population. The Commonwealth embraces countries at almost every stage of economic development, but its diversity is a strength, not a weakness. The process of understanding each other's problems can only benefit from the frank and informal exchange of opinions which a shared language and a shared history make possible.

We have established a democratic system and a tradition of political stability of which we in this country remain justifiably proud. By 1980 we shall be self-sufficient in oil and we will for the next few decades be the only major industrialised nation which is self-sufficient in energy. We have developed a way of life culturally and morally which is not only one of our most valued national assets, but is also a long-standing source of influence within Europe and on the world.

These positive strengths are too readily overlooked at home and abroad. Of course, there is a negative side too, which no one but a fool would ignore. In today's world we can no longer rely on the natural advantages of our insular position to safeguard what we value. With the growth of interlocking relationships, we in Britain find ourselves increasingly limited in our ability to protect our interests on our own. We are of course not unique in this.

We live in a world in which probably no nation, and certainly no industrialised nation, can any longer guarantee its prosperity and security without regard to the outside world. This in essence is what we mean by the vogue term 'interdependence'. It is interdependence which has, since 1945, transformed the international context in which British foreign policy has to operate. The central task of our foreign policy is to decide how best we can realise our fundamental objectives — to promote national prosperity and to safeguard national security — in an interdependent world.

We have first to recognise the link between prosperity and security. Prosperity is of little use without security. Our reliability as an ally and our capacity to play a useful role in the world are infinitely more difficult to sustain if we are economically weak.

We are increasingly vulnerable to decisions taken far from our shores, and over which we have little, if any, control. Our exports of goods and services represent something like one-third of our gross national product. We import half our food and even more of our raw materials. Developments in the international economy can and do, therefore, have a direct impact on the prosperity of every inhabitant of this country.

Since 1945, the management of national economies has become almost as much an area of international, as of domestic, decision-making. The industrialised democracies have a common interest in stable currencies, the expansion of free trade and the overriding need to avoid a repetition of the slump which took place so tragically in this country and in others in the 1930s. The world economic crisis since 1973 has underlined still further this mutual dependence.

World economic recovery depends first and foremost on an expansion of demand in the stronger economies of the world. A central economic issue is what to do about the OPEC surpluses. Then there is the problem of unemployment: increasingly structural and long-lasting, not cyclical; increasingly an international, not a national, phenomenon.

An important aspect of economic interdependence which is of equal concern is the relationship between the developed and developing worlds. The fundamental and most intractable features of this relationship are that in the international economy one-third of the world's population has a per capita income of less than £100 per annum; and that the present population of the developing countries is likely to increase by 60 per cent before the end of the century.

But the gap between rich and poor countries is not simply a matter of statistics. It is supremely a moral question which demands a firm and principled stand. It is even a question of security. Gross and ever-increasing inequalities are in the world at large, as they are in our own national societies, a source of confrontation and ultimately of open conflict. We are committed to working for a more fair and rational world economic system which will offer the people of the poorer countries the possibility of lives no longer dominated by malnutrition, want or chronic insufficiency. The fact that it is simply not possible, within the framework of national consent, to meet the demands of the less developed countries either immediately or all at once does not diminish the force of our commitment.

Increasingly since 1945, Britain has been voluntarily placing herself in common decision-making structures with other nations. This has meant compromise; not always getting one's way; but also achieving through common effort solutions to common problems which on our own we, like other nations, would be incapable of solving. This applies in particular to our membership of NATO and of the European Community.

The formation of NATO in 1949 reflected the fact that individually the states of Western Europe could not defend themselves, and that security could lie only in collective effort made with the United States. The relationships of Britain and Europe with the United States are an integral feature of the interdependent world in which British foreign policy operates. This is the logical consequence of the United States's position in the international economy. It also reflects the United States's military strength. Anglo–United States relations rest on the strongest of foundations: shared ideals and shared principles. It has never been for Britain a choice of Europe or the United States. We need both, and the United States needs both of us.

Membership of NATO is the foundation of British security. The Organisation is as essential in an age of detente as it was during the Cold War. For detente without security is a contradiction in terms. Fortunately, the basic feature of this particular aspect of Europe's relations with America is its reassuring stability, despite rapid change in international affairs. It is remarkable that after three decades of peace and profound economic and social changes, the Atlantic Alliance — an association of fifteen free and democratic nations — should still be strongly united and confident in its common objectives.

The Alliance is committed to detente, and to the continuing search for a more constructive, more manageable and safer relationship with the Soviet Union and the other countries of Eastern Europe. It would, however, be a serious error to see detente as an exclusively European process or one confined to a bilateral relationship between the two superpowers. There are a number of areas outside Europe where tensions present a chronic threat to world peace. The future credibility of detente depends on the restraint and responsibility of all states in their approach to crises inside and outside Europe. This is what we mean by the indivisibility of detente. Disarmament and arms control lie at the core of detente and are an essential part of any extension of human rights towards a safer world.

Britain joined the European Community at the beginning of 1973 because we realised that no single European nation had the resources, moral or material, successfully to overcome the challenges of the modern world. We saw that in the second half of the twentieth century Western European relationships would have to be placed on a wholly new footing and that Britain could not stand aside from this process. If the peoples of Western Europe were to progress in prosperity and peace; if the values of democratic societies were to withstand the pressures of threatening ideologies; and if Europe were to regain its proper place and influence in the world, a new spirit of co-operation, with new institutions to match, would have to arise in Europe. This is why we subscribed to our partners' determination expressed in the Treaty of Rome 'to lay the foundation of an ever closer union among the peoples of Europe ... ensure the economic and social progress of our countries by common action ... and pool our resources to preserve and strengthen belief in liberty'.

On 31st December 1977 the transitional period of Britain's European Community membership came to an end and, from the beginning of 1978, Britain has been a full member of the Community. This is true not only from a narrow legalistic point of view. These early years have seen a gradual adjustment to Community membership of approaches and practices in a whole series of fields of Government policy; but, much more profoundly, after a period—at times painful—of adjustment, there is now in Britain a new political understanding of the permanence of our EEC membership.

The Community of Nine is more than the Community of Six with three new members; the Community of Nine is a fusion which, even though the basic institutional framework has remained the same, has created a new Community. The new Community is something more than the sum of its component parts. Because Britain is the largest of the new members, we inevitably become the butt of the purists who wish to preserve unchanged the attitudes and practices of the Community of Six and see the Nine as no different from the original Six. They feel at times that Britain is trying to alter the Community to suit its own interests rather than conforming to the rules of the club which we joined voluntarily. Of course we must accept the rules; but the rules of a club can remain while the club changes its character, and this is what has happened in the Community.

The introduction of Political Co-operation in 1972 outside the framework of the Treaties has meant that the political development of the Community has increased while its institutional and financial development has slowed at least temporarily, perhaps because of the world economic recession. In pursuit of policies over human rights, the Community attempts to act together. We co-ordinate our voting pattern in the United Nations so that over 80 per cent of the time the Community has voted together. We co-ordinate our positions prior to and during conferences, as we did for the Helsinki Final Act and the follow-up conference in Belgrade.

Stability in Europe cannot be isolated from world stability. The Community has demonstrated its conviction that there is justice in the demand of the developing world for a more equitable economic order. Like us, France, Germany, Belgium and Holland have a colonial past and, like us, they see it as a vital interest of both the developed and developing nations that the latter should have their rightful influence in the international economic system. The Community, through the Lomé Convention covering fifty-two developing countries, has recently allowed human rights considerations to influence its policy, for example towards Uganda. However, there are limits to how far the Convention can be used, since it is based on the principle of equal participation and there has to be agreement between all parties.

The Community, which is, inevitably, concerned for the less fortunate amongst its own people, has accepted that it has an inescapable moral obligation to show a similar concern for the disadvantaged of the world, and that we cannot abandon the world's poor to the mercies of the Malthusian trilogy of war, famine and disease. Though the European Community started as a Common Market, its record is of active intervention and not relying solely on market forces. European socialists at least cannot with conviction use the language of social democracy at home and that of Adam Smith or *laissez-faire* in the international economy.

Whatever the political philosophy of its member states it has always been agreed that the Community has a duty to promote human rights and to deploy its political and economic influence to promote the dialogue with the developing world. This is in keeping not only with the long-standing ties of friendship and co-operation which individual member states enjoy outside Europe, but with the rapidly developing role of the Community itself as a force in international affairs.

23

Additionally, Britain pursues a universal, multilateral approach to human rights through the UN. The organisation has already achieved a great deal. Human rights are an integral part of the Charter itself. The Universal Declaration of Human Rights, approved by the UN in 1948, is generally regarded, and rightly so, as a standard text. The two International Covenants —one on economic, social and cultural rights, the other on civil and political rights—have given detailed expression to the Declaration's concept of man as a political, social and economic being. Enough states have ratified the Covenants to bring them now into force. The Human Rights Committee, set up specifically to supervise the implementation of the International Covenant on Civil and Political Rights, is functioning well. In addition, there is the machinery under the aegis of the Economic and Social Council (the Human Rights Commission, the Sub-Commission on Prevention of Discrimination and Protection of Minorities, the confidential procedure set up under Resolution 1503). We also have the useful human rights activities of the ILO and UNESCO. But, at the end of the day, the UN's only power of enforcement lies in the willingness and good faith of its members, qualities which are all too frequently absent from the organisation's consideration of human rights abuses. This would still be the case even if improvements of the kind which we in Britain favour were introduced: for instance, the appointment of a High Commissioner for human rights and more frequent meetings of the Human Rights Commission to provide greater continuity than at present exists. This is not an argument for going back on Britain's commitment to support the UN in every way possible. On the contrary, the abuse of human rights is a global phenomenon and it is on a global basis that the international community must try to progress: the UN alone provides a vehicle for this kind of approach. But we have to realise that progress will be slow and painful and that the ultimate goal of formally binding and enforceable commitments on member states in respect of universally agreed human rights criteria is something which must await our children or grandchildren.

Recently Nigeria introduced a resolution in the UN General Assembly in favour of regional commissions on human rights.

Britain welcomed this initiative. We did so because, if properly constituted and with the right kind of powers, regional commissions could assist the work of the UN. There is a lot to be said for complementing the global approach with one which makes allowance, within reason, for different traditions and different cultures. Certainly there seems to be a far greater chance of more effectively enforcing human rights if the countries in question share a reserve of common values.

This judgment is based primarily on our assessment, as a member of the Council of Europe, of the growing effectiveness of the European Convention on Human Rights and Fundamental Freedoms, which came into being in 1950, and of the instruments which enforce it: the European Commission on Human Rights—which for many years has had a British President—and the European Court of Human Rights. While the Convention owes a great deal to the Universal Declaration of Human Rights, it is unique in having enforcement machinery in the Commission and the Court which legally binds the member states of the Council of Europe. It provides for action either by an individual against a state or by one state against another.

We in Britain are as aware as any member of the Council of Europe of the real effectiveness of its human rights machinery because we have been taken to the Court and to the Commission both by states and by individuals. Most of the actions involving the UK have proved to be ill-founded; a few have not. The experience may not be particularly comfortable for us; but Britain accepts that the human rights machinery provided for under the European Convention has become an integral part of that empirical process by which over the centuries individual liberties in Britain have been expanded and reinforced. This process is the foundation of our democratic way of life. Unlike mainland Europe, with its traditions rooted in Roman law, we have never favoured formal constitutions, and there has been a reluctance to accept the arguments for a Bill of Rights. We have preferred instead to rely on Anglo-Saxon empiricism, building up step-by-step a body of law which will safeguard the rights of citizens. By definition this has to be a process of constant evolution to match society's equally continuous process of development. There will always be room for improvement in safeguarding the rights of the individual in Britain, as elsewhere in Europe; that the authority and meticulous standards of the Court and Commission are now engaged alongside our own national institutions in helping us to make these improvements is something wholly to be welcomed, not treated with insular suspicion. Applications lodged with the Commission or the Court in Strasbourg have, for instance, contributed to the establishment in the UK of a new system of appeals for immigrants entering the country and new regulations about the right of prisoners to have access to the courts.

What can or should be done to make the European Convention even more effective? The system has, of course, been subject to constant development over the years. The First and Fourth Protocols to the Convention added substantive new rights. A number of technical improvements have been made. Work is in hand on the more effective application of basic standards to particular problems relating, for instance, to press freedom and to the threat to privacy posed by data-processing banks. An inter-governmental committee of experts on which the UK is represented is currently exploring the possibility of adopting certain rights embodied in the International Covenant on Civil and Political Rights which are not explicitly covered by the European Convention.

At present the Convention is not fully implemented and not all the member states accept all its provisions and those of its Protocols. Four countries do not accept the compulsory jurisdiction of the Court. Five do not recognise the right of individual petition. Eight have not ratified the Fourth Protocol, including Britain, although we have signed it. This Protocol guarantees certain rights relating to the liberty of the person and to freedom of movement. At the back of this issue is a fundamental difference of outlook which is reflected in British attitudes, not just to the Council of Europe, but to the future development of the European Community.

A major difference of approach between ourselves and most of our European Community partners concerns the old division between the Anglo-Saxon and the Napoleonic philosophical and political traditions. The Napoleonic tradition, rooted in Roman law and the French Revolution, lays stress on setting out objectives and goals within a formal legal framework, while our own Anglo-Saxon tradition is one of empiricism, of building slowly, step by step. Fully-fledged federalism within the European Community is a noble goal but one which for most of us in Britain is unrealistic, and to some mythical. It is hard to generalise and there are many different views in Britain, but in the main the British outlook is practical. We cannot see in concrete terms how nine nations with very different political, social and cultural traditions — some of them still young nations in European terms — can possibly become federated over any timescale of political activity on which it is realistic to focus. Successful and self-sustaining federations have mostly developed over a long period, as in the US, or reflect considerable homogeneity as in Australia or Germany. While others speak in rhetorical terms, our instinct is to look at the practical consequences: total control of foreign policy, currency, monetary policy, the armed forces would all pass to a new supranational or federal Government. How soon are our partners really prepared to see that? Our approach is to seek practical improvements to immediate issues rather than to aim at a far-off goal for which hardly any of the necessary pre-conditions exist. The Treaty itself never spelt out the goal of a federal Europe; it defined the political objectives of the Community as 'to lay the foundations of an ever closer union among the peoples of Europe'. The British people prefer an evolving, open-ended Community and will resist, for sound cultural as well as political reasons, attempts to force the Community into a rigid, predetermined view of what a future Europe should be.

The founding fathers of the European Community in the early 1950s had as their aim a centralised Community in which the Commission would ultimately evolve into the Government of a united Europe. They believed that a federal structure would one day emerge from the Community and inevitably therefore the Treaty's institutional structure had a centripetal bias.

In fact, events have shown that — even if it were desirable, which many doubt — one cannot dissolve within two decades national interests and traditions which in some cases, like our own, have had more than a thousand years of uninterrupted development. Running against any federalist aspirations are the continuing power of national sentiment, varying national interests and national perceptions and, regrettably, economic divergence within the Community.

If one compares the history of Western Europe with the history of the United States, one can appreciate just how far we would have to go, even if we wanted a federal Europe. The United States developed a federal system in a society that was relatively homogeneous, both culturally and socially. The thirteen original states had a common language and a common cultural, historical and judicial background. They came together against a common enemy and continued together in the face of a common challenge—that of the vast and largely empty continent in which they lived. It took a devastating civil war nearly a century after the founding of the republic to confirm the federation, which developed geographically and demographically in slow and measured steps.

If one rejects federalism, how does one define the Community of the future? *Confederalism* is a term which is frequently used and some commentators have seen the Labour Government's attitudes as *confederalist*. The Community today, looked at objectively, could be defined as a confederal system; one where sovereign states cede to a central authority the responsibility for handling certain common matters, while retaining a measure of control over common business, and undisputed authority over everything for which responsibility has not been transferred to the centre. As a statement of fact, that is what the Community is, and as such it is acceptable.

'Confederalism' is open to the opposite criticism of 'federalism'—while 'federalism' contains a very clear notion of what future developments should be, 'confederalism' provides no idea of what its goal is and contains no clear notion of what should be handled collectively and what nationally. There is no confederation in existence today which provides a goal or model for the Community. Yet the strength of the Community is precisely that it is a completely new phenomenon. It does not follow any existing doctrinal blueprint, nor is it attempting to imitate any existing model.

The Community is a far cry from a normal intergovernmental organisation. In particular, it includes an institution—the Commission—which is much more than a simple secretariat. The independent role of the Commission is an important element in the way the Community works at present; and it is this element which distinguishes the Community from all other systems by which nation states are associated.

In Britain, it is felt with some justice that it has taken longer than we expected for parts of the Community—including parts of the Commission—to realise that Britain's being an island is a fact of geology and geography and not a reprehensible act of anti-Europeanism. It has not always been realised that an island nation will, quite justifiably, have an outlook of its own, for example, on fishing, just as a country rich in agricultural land like France has its own well-safeguarded outlook on agriculture. Or, to take another example, our water supply and pollution problems are quite different from those of our Continental neighbours. The fact that our rivers are shorter and faster-flowing than the great slow rivers of the Continent means that it is common sense for Britain to resist the imposition of harmonised standards based on the pollution problems of the Continental rivers.

An effective and efficient Commission providing the motor for carrying out policies, and setting common practices and standards where they are in all our interests, must adapt to the sheer practical difficulties of harmonising in a Community which has grown from six to nine. It will be even more necessary to adapt for a Community of twelve. The purists see enlargement as weakening the Community and even suspect the advocacy of enlargement as part of a strategy designed to weaken and destroy it. Enlargement will change the Community, and it is absurd to believe otherwise. One of the reasons the original Six pondered so long and hard over enlargement was their anxiety as to whether the gains would outweigh the losses. A Community of Six had great attractions, but also considerable limitations. It was because of its limits, particularly political limits, that the decision was taken to enlarge. The Community of the Nine similarly finds that it is political arguments and political pressures that are the main driving force behind the wish to enlarge to twelve.

There are limits to how much political considerations can override economic considerations. The basic cement for the Community comes from the fact that it was built up on the solid economic framework of coal, steel, trade tariffs and agriculture. No one is prepared to risk enlargement's undermining this essential basic framework. The Community is not just a political superstructure. It has important foundations protected by the Treaties and it is right that these should be safeguarded. There are already worrying trends showing economic divergence between the existing member states. If enlargement were to exacerbate these divergencies then it would damage the Community. If such a trend became firmly established, it would of itself seriously weaken the political and social cohesion of the Community.

Our support for the concept of enlargement is based on our strong political commitment to the support of democracy in Greece, Portugal and Spain. We believe that Community membership would, for these three countries, be an important factor in stabilising and protecting their democracy. We strongly advocate enlargement for political reasons but we are under no illusions about the economic and institutional problems that are certain to arise.

Enlargement is historically inevitable and politically desirable. Some of the applicant countries have been outside the mainstream of Western democratic development for two generations. The political imperative is thus undeniable.

The Community must, however, face the realities that flow from this political commitment. Enlargement will be difficult. It will widen the economic disparities already existing within the Community of Nine. It will slow down the process of convergence. It may make decisions harder to arrive at. It will certainly cost money; and it will impose strains on the economic and social structures of the three until the process of integration is completed.

Britain will continue to be as impatient with the architectural theories about the future of Europe as we are keen to take solid steps forward in the construction of a genuinely democratic

European partnership. And our partners must know that we do not have to define our objectives in what to us are theoretical and semi-theological terms in order to be good Europeans.

The Community is a unique structure and its development will have a very important influence on the future of this country and Europe. It is an economic institution, but with a developing political personality. It is an institution that combines elements of domestic and external policy. It is an institution with an inbuilt dynamism which has no parallel in any other international organisation.

It is vital that the Council of Europe and the European Community complement each other's work in the human rights field. The nine member states of the Community, singly and collectively, work hard to help create an international environment hostile to those who violate human rights. The strength of the Nine, which the more disparate members of the Council of Europe cannot and should not try to match, lies in their ability through the mechanism of political co-operation to speak and act as one on the international stage of human rights. This the Nine have done, for instance, at successive negotiations in the Conference on Security and Co-operation in Europe process and also in their outright condemnation of apartheid. On the other hand, the great virtue of the twenty-member Council of Europe is that it casts its net far wider than the EEC, to cover virtually all non-communist Europe. As the Community enlarges from nine to twelve, the broad membership of the Council of Europe ensures that states joining the EEC will have already entered into legally binding commitments on human rights under the European Convention, so buttressing the Community's democratic and human rights commitment.

There has been some duplication of effort between the Council and the Community in human rights matters. The main institutions of the Community—the Parliament, Council and Commission—produced last year a Joint Declaration on Fundamental Rights; in effect a statement of political faith. The Parliament has also called for the uniform application throughout the Community of civil and political rights guaranteed by the Court of Justice of the European Communities.

Since 1974 a working group of the Council of Ministers has been looking into the question of granting EEC nationals residing in other member states certain special rights. There has been a proposal for a justiciable Community Charter of Fundamental Rights. Up to a point this is all to the good; human rights are an issue of such basic importance that a little duplication of effort could be beneficial. But attempts by the Community to develop its own views should not be allowed to detract from the authority of the Council of Europe in human rights matters. It would, for instance, be a recipe for confusion, detrimental to the authority and prestige of the bodies concerned, still more to the cause of human rights itself, if certain member states found themselves answerable to the European Court in Luxembourg, as well as to the Court of Human Rights in Strasbourg.

The Convention probably represents the highest common factor of what can be collectively achieved in Europe at present. By contrast, some of the ideas which have been floated within the Community for uniform and judicially enforceable human rights standards presuppose a degree of uniformity which simply does not exist and would take many years to evolve. This may also be one of the main difficulties to face the French proposal for a common judicial area which the European Council recently agreed to study, and which provides for such matters as the transfer of criminal proceedings from one country to another and the reciprocal enforcement of criminal judgments. This is certainly something which should be seriously considered — the fight against international terrorism, one of the main objectives of this proposal, is a major concern of us all — but we shall need to know in detail what it entails before reaching any final conclusion.

Can we establish an order of priority between different categories of human rights; for instance, between political and civil rights, on the one hand, and economic and social rights, on the other? This poses problems of the greatest moral and political complexity which exercise academics, human rights experts and politicians alike.

The Social Charter of the Council of Europe, which sets out a number of social and economic rights and which the UK was the first to ratify, does not fall under the enforcement machinery of the European Convention. There have been suggestions that the Social Charter should be so protected. But it is central to the European system of protection that rights brought within the competence of the European Convention should be enforceable by the individual, that is to say, justiciable. In the nature of things, and with the best will in the world, many economic and social rights cannot be enforced simply by court order: poverty and unemployment would have been abolished long ago if that were the case. This must therefore limit any expansion of the scope of the Convention in this direction. None of this reflects a lack of concern on the part of the UK or the other Western democracies for the protection of economic and social rights either in their own countries or elsewhere. A parallel difference of approach is to be found in the UN and in the different ways in which the two International Covenants are implemented. While it has been possible to set up the Human Rights Committee to supervise the protection of civil and political rights, no procedure has yet been devised to supervise the implementation of economic, social and cultural rights.

The complex of human rights is morally indivisible. We must try and implement them all with equal vigour and determination. But in the nature of things, some of the economic and social rights are longer-term goals, if only because their attainment can be affected by forces outside the control of Government and of individuals. Furthermore, while the rights to work, to eat, and to enjoy an adequate standard of living and the support of social services are fundamental, they can have little meaning or purpose in societies where life itself is cheap, where the rule of law is imperfect or arbitrary, or turns a blind eye to torture, where by the denial of freedom of thought and expression in all its forms man loses the full use of his reason — the faculty which above all distinguishes him as a human being. It is no justification for apartheid that in South Africa the black population enjoys a higher standard of living than elsewhere in Africa. The demands of economic development are not such that, in any country, developed or developing, they justify setting aside basic political freedoms and civil rights. To deny

33

this proposition can only lead in strict logic to justifying dictatorship on the long since discredited grounds that it is economically
more efficient than democracy. We in Europe know only too
well where that argument leads.

3

Soviet Communism

Soviet ideology in relation to human liberty has led to inevitable tension between our Governments and our peoples. The Cold War marked the high point of mutual hostility between East and West. Since 1953 the two sides have tried instead to build a more constructive and less dangerous relationship. The initial steps were hesitant and there were rebuffs. At the time of Cuba, in Mr Khrushchev's graphic phrase, 'The smell of burning hung in the air.' But there were also genuine steps forward: for instance the 1963 Test Ban Treaty and the 1968 Nuclear Non-Proliferation Agreement. Slowly East and West came to recognise a common interest in the management of their relations to avoid military confrontation and nuclear war. On this foundation a variety of building blocks have since been put into place which today form the structure we recognise as detente.

No one with a grain of sense would deny the basic proposition that as a result of the detente process — a process which began almost twenty-five years ago and to which successive American Presidents and leading statesmen in all parts of Europe have contributed — East-West relations are more stable and the world safer. The *quantity* of nuclear weapons on both sides has regrettably increased in this period. But there has been a *qualitative* improvement in the way in which East and West seek to manage the mutual threat presented by each other's nuclear arsenals.

We have replaced the crude and arbitrary approach of the 1940s and 1950s with relatively sophisticated techniques for managing relations. This applies not only to the superpowers but also to relations between the countries of Europe, East and West.

It is most crucially reflected in the relationship between the

US and the Soviet Union. Few people realise that between 1971 and 1974 something like twenty-five bilateral agreements were signed between the United States and the Soviet Union, all contributing in a variety of ways to the development of a more stable relationship. The central achievement has been the willingness of the US and the Soviet Union to engage in talks on strategic arms limitation — to exchange views and data, and to try and reach agreement, in areas of the most advanced military technology. As a result there is today less risk of misunderstanding, less risk of military confrontation and therefore less risk of nuclear catastrophe.

Britain's commitment to detente and the search for a more constructive relationship with the Soviet Union and Eastern Europe is as firm today as it was on the eve of the conference in 1975 which resulted in the Helsinki Final Act. The Final Act, which sets out in black and white certain basic human rights, has been signed and published by thirty-five Governments, including those of the Warsaw Pact. But over the last two years or so a widespread feeling has developed in the West that too little has changed for the better and that some important things may even have changed for the worse.

No objective observer can deny that the Warsaw Pact continues to increase the effectiveness of its armed forces — on land, sea and air — and that this process has gathered momentum in the period of detente. Many rightly ask what all this military effort is for. Many also rightly ask whatever happened to the Seventh Principle of the Final Act, pledging signatory states to uphold human rights and fundamental freedoms. What has happened to the commitment to the free exchange of peoples and ideas, into which the thirty-five states have entered, and which remains more an aspiration than a reality?

As a result, and especially in the aftermath of the disappointing Belgrade follow-up conference, public opinion in the West has tended to display an increasing scepticism both towards the Final Act and by extension towards the process of detente itself. But it is equally true that some of this scepticism and disappointment has been misconceived; and that expectations have out-stripped by far the limits of what detente could have reasonably delivered.

36

For while detente has substantial achievements to its credit, the process started from a low threshold and represents to date only a limited, though vitally important, accommodation in Europe and between the superpowers. We are witnessing the early stages of this process, not its culmination. Detente has solved some of the most urgent and obvious problems in East-West relations and it has established a basic framework for the solution of those which remain. But there is still a long way to go.

The blunt truth is that the first and easier stage of detente is over. The issues which are today on the agenda of East-West relations are more complex, more contentious and far more intractable. We are beginning to encroach on fundamental attitudes, on human behaviour, and the issues go to the heart of each side's perception of itself and its interests. Inevitably we cannot expect to maintain the momentum of the early 1970s.

This makes it all the more important that we should be realistic. Detente on its own could not, and was never intended to, stop the Soviet Union from being a world power, still less to convert the Russians and their allies from communism. Already in the last century it was clear that it was only a matter of time before a country of the size, population and resources of Russia emerged as a global power. Any idea that detente could or should have reversed this process is absurd. The basic premise from which we in the West must start is that the Soviet Union is a world power with national interests and ambitions to match, which inevitably bring it into competition, and sometimes confrontation, with the West. To this we must add that communist ideology invests the natural rivalry between East and West with a dynamic of unceasing struggle.

Increasingly, as we have devised mechanisms for reducing military tension, this struggle has become one for the minds of men. There is no armistice in the war of ideas. But this is a struggle from which we have no reason to shrink. Why else do we permit a free flow of information and ideas in both directions? We are confident that our model of society is better adapted to satisfy human aspirations, both intellectual and material. True, we in the West have our problems. But they are of a complexity and sophistication which communist

37

societies are only just beginning to encounter. Above all Western society thrives on the intellectual ferment and the unfettered expression of human creativity in all its forms.

So, sweeping away the unreal expectations and delusions of recent years, we see that detente so far has to be placed in the context of a relationship in which competition between the two systems exists side by side with the search for common ground. The scope for accommodation between East and West is limited by this competition. Some ask whether it is worth our while to try and expand the limits.

The answer must be emphatically 'yes'. The present relationship is essentially unstable. It still carries the risk of miscalculation and disaster. We have to reduce this risk even further.

But, as we try and open up the frontiers of East-West understanding, the Jekyll and Hyde nature of detente — competition on the one hand, co-operation on the other — will constantly assert itself. This is not something which we should try and sweep under the carpet. Both sides have everything to gain from frankly and openly facing up to the consequences of their differing perceptions of detente. In the last analysis this offers East and West the best long-term hope of progressively reducing the area of confrontation between them; and of progressively increasing the area of common ground. It would be folly indeed for one side to make the process of detente so distasteful to the other that it would prefer to opt out altogether. The golden rule must be that neither side should pursue policies which so raise the level of confrontation that the structure of detente is itself threatened.

This is, of course, easier said than done. Detente is an immensely complex process, comprising innumerable strands and relationships on different levels: political dialogue, commercial and technological exchange, cultural contacts, ideological debate and military vigilance. There is no magic formula which will enable us, East or West, to strike the right balance in our relations at all times. Both sides are still feeling their way. All we can say is that balance there must be between the elements of confrontation and co-operation, whether we are talking of the detente process as a whole or of its constituent parts.

Among the elements of competition is what the communist countries call the 'ideological' struggle. It is important to establish the relationship between detente and the so-called ideological struggle; to try to understand what is meant by the term; and in the process to define certain features of detente.

The Russians tell us that detente applies only to relations between Governments. It cannot alter or abolish the laws of the class struggle. Detente creates an international climate in which, so they say, the ideological struggle can not only be prosecuted, but prosecuted more effectively.

The so-called ideological struggle—although there are good grounds for preferring the word 'competition'—manifests itself in two ways: one which is acceptable to us and one which is not. The acceptable and true ideological struggle is the free competition of ideas: competition between the communist way of life, founded on collectivism, totalitarian philosophy, and the absolute sway of a single party in the Soviet Union and, in varying degrees, in Eastern Europe; and the parliamentary, democratic way of life, founded on individual liberties and free institutions which allow full play to the development of the human personality. In the 1960s, theories about the growing convergence of the two ways of life were widely held. But they failed to look beyond the emerging consumerism and the new bourgeoisie of Eastern Europe to what were, and remain, fundamental differences between East and West.

It is a paradox that detente heightens the competition between the two ways of life. As contact and communication grow between countries and peoples in the East-West dialogue, so the system on each side faces fundamental challenges from the system on the other. The Western side has nothing to fear from this. We are not without serious problems of our own, not least those posed by economic recession. But despite the immense challenge which unemployment and inflation present in our countries—with which we are still grappling—willingness to listen to criticism, to recognise shortcomings, is not only one of the hallmarks of our society, it is an essential ingredient of human progress. Believing this, we should enter the competition of ideas full of confidence.

The Eastern side, on the other hand, tends to be afraid of

this competition and tries to circumscribe it and prevent it from being competition in any truly free sense. Hence their predilection for certain one-sided rules of the detente game, the main purpose of which is to limit the scope for the freer exchange of ideas in Eastern Europe by insisting on state control of contacts between individuals and organisations, by labelling the West's approach to detente as a threat to Soviet and East European sovereignty, and by insisting that the West is breaking the rules on non-interference in internal affairs.

'Ideological struggle' becomes unacceptable to the West where it is used as a cloak for the prosecution of destabilising policies, particularly in the Third World, in the interests of promoting Soviet power and influence. The Soviet Union would doubtless argue that anything which advances Soviet influence advances the cause of communism and is therefore legitimate. We would argue that while every power has a right to work for the improvement and consolidation of its relations with other countries, whether in the Third World or elsewhere, the methods adopted and the underlying objectives deserve to be carefully considered and are bound to have a direct effect on that country's credibility in the eyes of the rest of the world. The world we stand for is pluralistic: one in which all our people are, individually and collectively, free to control their own destinies; free to choose their own systems of government and to change their Governments when they wish; free to shape their own societies; free, if they wish, to change their frontiers by negotiations and peaceful agreement in accordance with international law; free to seek help from others or to refuse it; free to order their economies and their foreign trading policies in the directions they think most likely to promote their own well-being; free to choose public ownership or private ownership or a combination of both; free to move in or out of their frontiers; free to read or learn as they wish about anything, anywhere.

It is wholly unacceptable to us that any power should foster, exploit or aggravate unstable situations in order to extract advantage. Where that is seen to happen, it is inevitable that the credibility of that power's commitment to detente will be called in question. Irresponsible behaviour in areas beyond the boundaries of Europe and North America will have a direct effect on the way in which public opinion within Europe and North America evaluates the detente process.

There is another sense in which this application of the ideological struggle is unacceptable. By Third World standards the economies of Eastern Europe are developed. They, like us, have a responsibility to contribute to the transfer of resources which the poorer countries so desperately need. So far the performance of the communist countries has done nothing to suggest that they are yet aware of their full responsibilities. They tend to explain away their position by invoking outdated colonial arguments. Although we, the industrialised democracies, are ourselves in no position to boast—we could and should make a greater effort—we estimate that in 1975 the net aid disbursements of the Soviet Union and Eastern Europe to the Third World (excluding Vietnam and Cuba), amounted to less than 5 per cent of those of the industrialised democracies, whereas on any scale of equivalence related to GNP it should have been about 36 per cent.

Far too much of the aid that they do give is focused on arms and military equipment, and far too little on the basic economic needs of the developing world. If we are serious about alleviating poverty and inequality in the world, we must widen the North-South dialogue to include the communist countries, and others who are in a position to contribute generously and constructively. Ideological differences between East and West should not be allowed to stand in the way of this objective. This is potentially an area for co-operation. But it is an objective which will remain beyond reach as long as communist countries attach greater importance to the power struggle than to a co-operative and responsible approach to the crucial issue of world poverty.

Appalling and well-documented events rightly focus our attention on the abuse or absence of political, civil and legal rights; and on violations of the integrity of the person. But there is another category of rights for which we must also show concern: man's economic and social rights, the rights to freedom from chronic poverty, malnutrition and disease.

In the past twenty-five years, detente has been built on the steady progress made by East and West in managing the mutual threat presented by each other's nuclear weapons. The question now is whether the two sides can advance the detente process by placing within manageable bounds the mutual threat presented by the ideological struggle.

When we say that detente has to be worldwide, we mean precisely that the Soviet Union must give up its destabilising efforts in areas outside Europe and North America. This is an entirely justified demand provided that we accept that it applies to the West as well. Insistence on this principle is a necessary part of detente.

There can be no lasting and stable peace in the world if attempts to find peaceful solutions in different continents are sabotaged by other nations, either acting on behalf of major participants in the ideological struggle or encouraging solutions by force based on massive exports of modern or obsolescent weapons. The basic premise is that detente is indivisible and does not stop in Europe, Africa or Asia. It is right to resist destabilising acts in the name of detente wherever they occur.

Now the debate over human rights has posed a new question: to keep the mutual threat presented by the ideological struggle in bounds, should the West be circumspect in challenging the Soviet Union to free competition in the East-West dialogue?

The answer is not easy. Certainly the challenge should be made. The true ideological struggle is fundamental to detente and it has to be steadfastly pursued. Without it, detente would be no more than trade arrangements and a bureaucratically managed arms race with no creative contact between the two sides. Yet the fundamental point which has to be recognised is that it is no use asking for rapid change. This does not mean that it is necessary or desirable to see here the makings of a bargain, to draw up some kind of code of conduct, tacit or declared.

We must assert our Western values unhesitatingly; we should make it clear that we shall not compromise. But we must recognise that change involves human behaviour and that can come only by evolution. Behavioural change rarely comes rapidly; and even when it does, it is either so volatile that it only increases instability, or it carries the rigidity that so often goes with conversion and slows up the process of give-and-take inherent in any dialogue.

This argument applies with particular force to the human rights issue. It is in human rights that we find the values which underlie our societies and give sense to Western efforts in the ideological struggle. Unless the relaxation of tensions brings greater enjoyment of human rights, detente has no meaning or purpose beyond our immediate survival. We shall never have a world in which peace, stability and prosperity are the rule, not the exception, unless there is also respect for basic human rights and civil liberties.

The United States and the countries of Western Europe can all share this basic aspiration without having to adopt any particular uniform posture. Every country will have to make its own judgment, in terms of practical politics, on how best to register the concern of its public opinion at abuses of human rights. National interests, culture, history and geography will be the determining factors. And where human rights in Eastern Europe are concerned, we must also take into account differing interests in detente: differences which are by no means irreconcilable, but which should be seen rather as variations on a central theme.

But despite different nuances within the Western Alliance, a basic consensus exists. This was demonstrated in the united front displayed by representatives of the Western democracies during the Belgrade Review Conference.

Detente is a relationship in which competition between East and West exists side by side with the search for common ground: this is the central contradiction of detente and its central challenge. In consequence there are immutable realities which cannot be ignored. If detente is to prosper, there must be something in it for everyone; and if this is to happen, there must be balance between the elements of co-operation and conflict.

Western public opinion has made it plain that it will not support detente unless it advances the cause of human rights in Eastern Europe. On the other hand, a vital condition for championing human rights in Eastern Europe is the continuation of detente itself. Our task, if detente is to continue on lines acceptable to East and West, is to thread a difficult and delicate way between these two propositions. If we try to define a code of conduct we could introduce a complicating rigidity. In practice, this means that we must distinguish between our principles and the means we employ to put them into effect; and that we must then strike a balance between principles and means.

There is no going back on the human rights commitment. It is here to stay. Unless the Soviet leadership recognises that genuine public concern for human rights is a major determinant of Western foreign policy, the future of detente will be in doubt.

The balance between frank criticism and confrontation has been difficult to maintain, particularly during the review of past implementation. Strong emotions are aroused by some of the things which have been done, or not done, in apparently flagrant violation of the provisions of the Final Act. This of course applies most of all to the area of human rights. But if we are ever to make real progress in this area, the Western Governments will have to show patience and careful judgment. If we use the CSCE process as a vehicle for the uncontrolled venting of moral indignation, we risk destroying it. If we are to induce the Russians, for example, to refrain from the persecution of certain individuals, it may not necessarily be productive for Western Governments to challenge them openly and specifically by persistently naming those individuals and sponsoring their cases as if they were our own. In the British Government's view, it is better that the focus should be on categories of human rights cases and on the need for universal application of agreed standards of behaviour, rather than on individuals.

It is also important, if this emphasis on the principle of universality is to be convincing and effective, that those in the West who seek to put pressure on others in the field of human rights should not show any reluctance to discuss their own record in these matters, and that of their friends. The British Government's practice, as was made clear by the UK delegation at Belgrade, is to be fully ready to listen to any comment from others on its record on human rights matters, to accept criticism where it is fair, and to rebut it firmly where it is unjustified. This attitude was maintained, for instance, throughout the recent Irish state case brought against us by the Irish Government. We have always made it plain that if the facts show us to be in the wrong, we are willing to accept the verdict against us and to take any necessary remedial action.

The same principle of universality, it seems to me, has implications for human rights pressure groups. It is of course entirely right and understandable that, in fighting for human rights, Jewish groups should concern themselves mainly with Jews in communist countries; and we all respect the determination, persistence and ability to operate on an international scale which they show in making their views felt. But the fact that this concern is displayed so conspicuously and at times almost exclusively in the cause of Soviet Jewry does in my view tend to limit the effectiveness of the groups concerned and may even cause some resentment among those who are competing for public sympathy and support on behalf of equally deserving cases which do not involve Jews. The force of Jewish lobbying in this area would be greatly strengthened if it were quite consciously and visibly extended to cover other ethnic and religious groups, not only within the Soviet Union, but also elsewhere.

One of the reassuring aspects of the present situation is that innumerable contacts between East and West, themselves the direct result of detente, thrive to an extent which would have been impossible before the detente period. They embrace scientific and environmental co-operation, commercial and cultural exchanges, all kinds of academic contact, as well as a continuing political dialogue at ministerial and official levels.

These everyday contacts form a safety net on which East-West relations can, at least temporarily, rest.

In this way detente has established its own infrastructure and bureaucracy with a vested interest in the continuation of the process. Tried and tested ways of doing things have been evolved which are now familiar and acceptable to the bureaucracies on both sides. Barring a sharp and unforeseen deterioration on fundamental issues, there is in the bureaucratic processes of detente a certain assurance of measured, if unspectacular, progress.

But this is not enough. The lesson of the past twenty-five years is that without the repeated stimulus of a bold political input at the highest level there can be no qualitative advance in East-West relations. On the Western side, the highly personal contributions of American and European leaders have over the years left their mark on detente. Each of them in their different way—through summit meetings, personal contact, 'back-channel' diplomacy, and other means—turned the ratchet another notch, extending the area of co-operation and in the process raising East-West relations to a higher level. The statesmen of the world have a particular responsibility to engage themselves in detente. On the Soviet side, President Brezhnev can justly claim to have made a major and distinctive contribution.

The motor of detente is this dialectic between the bold political contribution and bureaucratic continuity. Both elements are essential to the process. But there must be balance between them. We must be very careful, when introducing a new political element, that it should not be so sharply at variance with what has gone before that the whole process snaps under the strain. The warning sounded by George Kennan in the *International Herald Tribune* is still relevant:

> To many people, the advantages of the present relationship may not seem large. But they represent the product of long and patient effort; and they rest, such as they are, on certain reassuring concepts of the motives and purposes of the other party which it has taken long to establish but which could be quickly shattered by confusing signals or abrupt changes in personality and behaviour at either end. Once shattered, these concepts could not be easily restored ...

These considerations apply with particular force to the Helsinki Final Act. While the Act marked an important stage in the development of co-operative relations between East and West there is no denying that several of its provisions contain the seeds of confrontation. It is important therefore that we should clearly understand its significance. The Final Act is not a treaty which has given the sanction of international law to the *status quo* in Europe. It is, on the contrary, a declaration of purpose which looks to the future, not to the past. It provides specifically for peaceful change. Its value is fundamentally long-term: as a charter and code of behaviour for what we hope will in time become a more normal and open relationship between both Governments and peoples in East and West. It reflects detente's highest aspirations.

Anyone judging the Final Act in terms of quantifiable, concrete results would conclude that progress so far has been extremely limited. But the Government never expected the provisions of the Final Act to be implemented immediately or all at once. Those in this country who have already dismissed the Final Act as not worth the paper on which it is written are at best short-sighted, at worst all too ready to substitute short-term political rhetoric for long-term political progress. In pressing for the implementation of the Final Act, we are in many areas dealing with entrenched attitudes which in the nature of things will not change overnight. But recent events in Europe have shown that the Final Act has already begun to be an inspiration and a point of reference for those who want to see their societies evolve peacefully and constitutionally in a more open direction. The signatories of Charter 77 in Czechoslovakia profess no wish to overthrow the regime; concern themselves strictly with freedom of speech and basic human rights; and all quote the Final Act. It is in the chords which it has spontaneously struck, without any outside assistance, in some of the countries of Europe that we see one of its most interesting and hopeful effects.

Given a consistent and well-thought-out political strategy for implementation, the objectives of the Final Act are capable of achievement. But there is no room for false optimism, for claiming breakthroughs on spurious evidence. The West was right not to claim a cosmetic victory at Belgrade. The results were meagre and it was best to say so, though the meeting itself had value in that it did subject the human rights record of communist countries to systematic examination. The public are not fools; they will judge detente by actual achievements, not political posturing.

To make progress over detente we must refine still further our techniques for managing crises between East and West.

This is not so much a matter of reaching specific agreements as of reducing to an absolute minimum the area of possible miscalculation between the two sides.

It means that we should be as well informed as possible of each other's intentions and preoccupations—and here high-level bilateral visits and contacts have an important role to play. Though we do not sell arms and restrict the passing of technological data we encourage trade and cultural links and welcome exchanges of view with Soviet and other Eastern European leaders. But these exchanges will be of strictly limited value unless both sides accept the basic premise that detente is indivisible and does not stop in Europe. We have made it plain to the Soviet Government that the continuing credibility of detente depends on the restraint and responsibility of all states in their approach to crises inside and outside Europe. Events in Angola, Zaire and the Horn of Africa, where the Soviet Union has used Cuba as a surrogate and shifted the military balance within the area to its advantage, are a serious development.

It is absurd to try and deny the Soviet Union any more than the United States the right to be involved in Africa or to advance its interests by the normal political, diplomatic and economic means. It is no part of the purpose of detente to deny the Soviet Union or anyone else its role as a world power, but we have the right to be concerned about how they deploy their influence and resources as a superpower, as they have the right to be concerned about us and our allies.

The Soviet Union and her allies, notably the Cubans, intervened in the fighting between Ethiopia and Somalia at the request of the Ethiopian Government. Whatever our misgivings about the scale and nature of this intervention—and they were considerable—and however serious our concern about some of the internal policies and practices of the Ethiopian regime, we could not deny the right of a sovereign African state to seek help from wherever it could when its territory was threatened. The West similarly accepted the right of President Mobutu of Zaire in 1977 and in 1978 to call in help from Morocco. The West should encourage African states to resolve among themselves the problems of Africa and any assistance should avoid extending African disputes into an

East-West confrontation but be firmly rooted in seeking an African solution.

This is why we could not support Somalia or supply them with arms while their troops remained in the Ogaden. The West has been criticised by some for not supplying arms, but this would have put us in direct conflict with the principles of the United Nations Charter as well as those of the Organisation of African Unity and would have damaged the West's long-term credibility and authority in Africa. Ironically, it was the same critics who advocated Western military intervention in Zaire. Ethiopia was warned by the West against any move to cross the Somali frontier, and it is a hopeful sign that Ethiopia in the aftermath of the fighting abided by the assurances given. The Russians and the Cubans also recognised the need for responsible action and the dangers of a real East-West confrontation if they attacked Somalia. The nature of the Soviet and Cuban intervention in the Horn of Africa placed a large question mark over the future of detente and risked a major escalation of the conflict.

There are other disquieting features about this intervention in Africa, not least the way it questioned the oft-repeated Soviet profession of a principled foreign policy and the Cuban claim to an independent foreign policy. Cuba claims a leading place in the Non-Alignment Movement. Yet had it not been for the Soviet Union investing so much military hardware in Somalia for so many years, far beyond the legitimate needs of national self-defence, the Somalis would never have been in a position to invade the Ogaden in the first place. The Soviet Union can claim, justly, to have ended the war, and it has been claimed by some in the West as a success for Soviet foreign policy. But it was a war which they had themselves fuelled with their own arms and was between two states which had both formerly been their friends. The outcome is hardly a creditable chapter in Soviet foreign policy.

The Soviet and Cuban attitude to the Eritrean Liberation Movements is equally open to question. For years the Cubans supported the Eritrean fighters with advice and training, presumably with Soviet encouragement. Then in 1978 the Eritreans were suddenly spoken of as pawns in the imperialists' game. The world saw in a very vivid way the extent to which the Cubans were Soviet surrogates and non-aligned countries began themselves to question the credentials of Cuba.

In Africa, we in the West are often criticised. We cannot dispute the fact that we have a colonial legacy, and that we have made mistakes. The legacy goes back a long time, to the Middle Ages, when Portugal, the Netherlands and other European countries first moved into parts of Africa, but one has to turn to the Middle Ages in Europe to find a parallel to what has happened in Africa since 1975; to the private armies who then moved around, tilting the military balance indiscriminately at the whim of feudal barons and at the beck and call of those who could pay and feed them.

Deploying military force in this way inevitably puts the emphasis on the violent settlement of disputes; it gives the potential for rapid disruption and it can suddenly shift the regional balance of power. It was estimated at one time that there were 16,000 Cuban and 1,000 Russian military personnel, including combat troops in the case of Cuba, in Ethiopia. There has been for some time a Cuban presence in Angola of 20,000, a large proportion military, and several hundreds elsewhere in Southern Africa. The overall size of the Cuban armed forces is some 400,000, including reserves and paramilitary units—4 per cent of the population. That is a very large proportion. As long as the Cuban forces remain in Africa, there will always be a temptation for them to use their forces in new situations. In Eritrea, their forces could have become involved in what was essentially a problem of internal security. No invading external force was involved.

The situation in Africa cries out for negotiated settlements with a minimum of further bloodshed. East-West relations are bound to be affected if it becomes clear that the Soviet Union and Cuba are actively committed, and on a massive scale, to military campaigns in what are essentially internal African affairs. The OAU has conciliated successfully in the past. The United Nations was heavily involved in the Eritrean problem in 1950 and in the Congo in 1956. Both should now raise their collective voices against any attempt to impose military solutions, and try hard to achieve negotiated solutions.

Even more serious complications for Africa and East-West relations would follow if there were any attempt to use Cuban forces or any other outside forces to undermine current talks to bring peace and democracy to Rhodesia and Namibia through negotiated and internationally acceptable settlements.

Detente should not be just about the absence of war and the avoidance of crises: it should tell us something about conditions of peace. This means that we should try and adopt a more coherent and systematic approach to all aspects of our relations. We must maximise our co-operation in areas of common interest: for instance, in the vital area of nuclear non-proliferation where Britain and the Soviet Union are both members of the Nuclear Suppliers Group—we must improve the stability of the East-West military balance. The emphasis must be on the discussions between the United States and the Soviet Union about further limitation of strategic arms, and on the talks between the two military alliances at Vienna about balanced force reductions in Europe. The need for greater military confidence between East and West lies at the core of detente.

We recognise that the issue of human rights is only one strand in the complex of East-West relations. It is no part of our policy to promote campaigns of denunciation or to assume the role of *agents-provocateurs*. Equally, the communist countries must recognise that concern for human rights is not a diversionary tactic but an integral part of foreign policy in the Western democracies.

In the last analysis it is the Government which must judge how best to give effect to the principles to which we all aspire; and inevitably different circumstances will require different measures. Yet, while the Government has to determine policy, unless the Government enjoys public support for its policies, those policies cannot be sustained. In a democracy no Government can or should ignore legitimate concern voiced by sections of public opinion over the plight of individuals in other countries who are deprived of basic human rights.

Equally the public must recognise that, in deciding how best to register this concern, Governments have to take into account the complexity of inter-state relations and the different levels on which these operate. This is not an excuse for dodging the issue:

it is the means by which we try to draw the fine line between measures that stand a chance of being effective, and those which will spark counter-productive reaction. In practice this means that sometimes private pressure may be more effective; at other times a strong public stand may be necessary.

At times the public declarations of Government will not be as exhilarating as, for instance, some of the highly articulate statements of famous exiles from Eastern Europe or elsewhere. Their message as an appeal to individual hearts and minds to stand up for humanity carries conviction. Their courage and also the generous response of individuals in our society to their appeal are a stimulant to us all. Governments may have a less declaratory message. For a Government's first task is to help provide and sustain the framework of peace and security within which human rights can be discussed, championed and enlarged. Open debate can only deepen understanding of these complex issues. The supporters of detente have everything to gain and nothing to lose from wide-ranging public discussion.

Whatever some may claim, there is nothing irreversible about detente. It is a permanent state of negotiation. It carries with it no built-in guarantee against failure or reversal. Unless we move forward we could place in jeopardy all the achievements of detente so far.

We in the West must do all we can to ensure not only that detente does not go into reverse but also that it broadens the area of common ground between East and West. This calls for goodwill and high negotiating skill. Above all it means that we in the West must be sure of ourselves: we must be secure in the cohesion of our alliances and partnerships; we must be secure in our faith in our own democratic institutions; and we must be secure in our ability to deter threats from whatever quarter. On this basis, we can make a contribution to detente, and co-operation and mutual confidence may reach a new level of achievement, to the benefit of all the peoples of Europe, West and East.

4

Communism in Western Europe

Today, for anyone concerned about human rights, there are few questions requiring a more urgent and considered answer than how to deal with the communist party in Western Europe. It is an urgent question because, in a number of countries, communist parties claim to have changed and, specifically, to have abandoned their subservience to Moscow and acquired a commitment to parliamentary democracy.

It used to be said that while communism has noble aims but evil methods, and fascism evil aims and evil methods, socialism has the distinction of combining noble aims and noble methods. The true values and beliefs of democratic socialism are based not, as its enemies maintain, on collectivism and bureaucracy, but on altruism and a commitment to a more equitable society. These values are combined with an unwavering support for the necessity to submit to the verdict of the ballot-box, born not out of reluctant acceptance but out of conviction and respect for the judgment of one's fellow beings. Democratic socialism dedicated to alleviating poverty and redressing inequality cannot base its appeal on self-interest. It relies for support on persuasion, not on coercion—on an appeal to the altruistic element in us all.

It is very easy for anyone committed to the philosophy of the left to conclude that a free electorate will never be persuaded by the emphasis on the disadvantaged minority. Therefore, some argue that it is permissible to forgo what could be regarded as the luxury of democracy. Many on the left who become communists justify their stance in such terms, believing that only a single party can push through essential reforms, and that only a single party can ensure the necessary discipline to put right the evils and inconsistencies in society. These authoritarian traditional marxist-leninist views are the antithesis of democratic socialism.

The power and influence of communist parties in a number of European countries has given added urgency to the question. In Italy, the Communist Party, with 34 per cent of the votes in the 1976 parliamentary elections and a long involvement in regional and local government, is now the second most powerful party. In Spain, Sñr Carrillo's defiance of the Soviet Union seems to be making him into a popular figure and the communists are major political rivals of the PSOE or democratic socialists. In France communist electoral support was sufficiently large for the socialists and left-radicals to have to reckon with it in forming the Left Coalition to fight the March 1977 elections.

In Britain, although Communist Party membership in July 1977 stood at only 25,293, the CP remains influential. In a whole series of fronts communists are active, not as communists used to be, advancing the claims of their party, building up their support in industry and attacking democratic socialists, but in the 'student broad left', as anti-racists, women's activists or community workers. This dangerous conscious blurring of the edges between communism and socialism—which has the *Morning Star* referring to MPs not as 'Labour' but as 'left' or 'social democrat'—puts the challenge to democratic socialists at a more insidious level. The challenge remains. In this new, modified, respectable form it is far more dangerous, for it presents a real risk of eroding the foundation stone of socialism's commitment to democracy.

As far as electoral power is concerned, the communists in this country remain a derisory force. Their total vote in the twenty-nine seats they contested in the October 1974 general election was 17,000. British communists—who discarded the concept of the 'dictatorship of the proletariat' and adopted the 'British road to socialism' in 1951—have signally failed to gain the support of the British people. The British Communist Party, like their comrades in France, Italy and Spain, have criticised the Soviet Union and voiced a commitment to respect parliamentary institutions. Yet they have never obtained the same electoral support. The reasons are complex — historical and philosophical — but they should be analysed with care.

The British Communist Party has solemnly declared that, if it attained power, 'democratically organised parties, including those hostile to socialism, would have the right to maintain their organisation, publications and propaganda, and to contest elections'. Do they mean this? Can we believe them? The same questions need to be asked in France, Italy and Spain. These three parties have made repeated, solemn and sometimes joint affirmations of their commitment to uphold the basic freedoms of pluralist, parliamentary democracy not only during the process of 'building socialism' but also after its consummation. They reject the Soviet path to communism as unsuitable for conditions in their own countries. For them the Soviet model, based as it is on the violent seizure of power in an early industrial society, in which the bourgeoisie formed only a tiny part of the population, is far removed from present-day conditions in Western Europe. Equally, they argue that the conditions in present-day Italy, France and Spain have nothing in common with the situation in Eastern Europe immediately after the last war when the physical presence of the Red Army was a decisive factor in creating communist regimes. In a report to the Central Committee of the PCI in 1975, Sig. Berlinguer said that it was 'unthinkable that socialism can be built in the West in the forms and ways in which it was achieved in Soviet Europe and in the other countries of Eastern Europe and Asia'.

'Eurocommunism' is a term invented by non-communists. It describes certain characteristics and attitudes which are shared by a number of Western European communist parties — notably the Italian, French and Spanish — and which became readily visible to the world at large for the first time during the preparations for the 1977 meeting of European communist parties in Berlin. Despite important political differences between the three main Eurocommunist parties — reflecting different levels of electoral support, different relationships with the respective socialist parties, and, more fundamentally, distinct national traditions, cultures and historical experiences — they have since come to accept the Eurocommunist label and on occasion to use it.

To these three parties the principle of separate national roads to socialism is fundamental: they therefore reject the leading role of the Soviet Communist Party in the world communist movement. At the same time they profess a similar diagnosis of advanced capitalist society and of their role in it. As Sig. Berlinguer has put it: 'What is being called Eurocommunism is the fruit of an elaboration that each of us has accomplished separately ... considering also what the developed countries of Western Europe have in common.' The three parties argue that the transformation of society from capitalism to socialism, by which they mean the creation of a communist society, requires their participation in the institutions and political processes of what they would call the bourgeois democratic state. In Western European conditions, only the parliamentary road can lead to political power. Since they assert that this transformation must enjoy the consent of the majority of the people, they seek alliances with non-communist political parties and, for themselves, broad-based electoral support going beyond their traditional constituency, the industrial working class.

This in turn has led to criticism of some of the features of contemporary Soviet and East European society and the way in which communism has developed in the Eastern European countries. The French, Italian and Spanish Communist Parties have all attacked the human rights records of the regimes in Eastern Europe and the Soviet Union. The Declaration of Freedoms adopted by the French Communist Party in 1975 not only covers all those which exist in pluralist democracies, but includes some, such as freedom from arbitrary confinement in mental institutions, which would never have been listed had they not been abused in the Soviet Union.

The central question is not whether, or to what extent, the communist parties in Europe are still marxist—leaving communist parties aside, marxist thought is in any case part of the intellectual inheritance of Western Europe and together with Methodism, guild socialism and anarchism, an important strand in Labour Party thinking. We have instead to ask ourselves what the attitude of these communist parties really is to democracy and to the ballot-box. At the Seventh Congress of the Comintern in 1935, Georgi Dimitrov, the Secretary General, said in launching a popular front policy, 'Comrades, you will remember the ancient tale of the capture of Troy ... We, revolutionary workers, should not be shy of using the same tactics.' Is communism in Europe a latter-day Trojan Horse for dictatorship and totalitarianism? Or has there been a qualitative change since the 1930s, as a result of which the major Western European communist parties have a genuine and lasting contribution to make to the further development of democracy within a framework of individual liberties and pluralist values?

The questions are unanswerable. The communist parties in question have yet to be put fully to the test of governmental responsibility and, unless and until they are, nobody, including even their leaders themselves, can be certain of what will happen. What is important is that we should try to understand clearly the nature of communism in Europe, as it has evolved so far, and to seek to establish in what direction it may be moving. In the meantime, the issue which divides democratic socialists from communists in Britain — that of a proven commitment to democratic values and institutions — must be regarded as equally relevant to our relationship with the communists on the Continent.

There have always been divisions on the left and in the Communist International. The debate between the Italian, French and Spanish parties, on the one hand, and those of the Soviet Union and Eastern Europe, on the other, is yet another example of the permanent tension between so-called revisionists and revolutionaries in the communist movement — a tension which can be traced back to and beyond the rift between Bolsheviks and Mensheviks in pre-revolutionary Russia, itself the precursor of the split between communism and social democracy.

Marx himself waged endless polemical battles with other European socialists: Bakunin in Russia, Proudhon in France, Lassalle in Germany, to name but a few. The First Socialist International saw the split between Marx and Bakunin, from which the anarchist movement developed.

The Second International collapsed in 1914 when the member parties broke with Lenin, rejecting the cause of international socialism and supporting their respective national Governments in the First World War. The Third, and first truly communist, International, founded in 1919 by Lenin when revolution seemed to be sweeping Europe, denounced bourgeois democracy, proclaimed the dictatorship of the proletariat and so formalised the breach with the social democrats. It was the Cominform, set up in 1947 to reassert Soviet control over the international communist movement in the Cold War, which provoked the split with the Yugoslav party a year later.

Since the last World Conference of Communist Parties in Moscow, divisive tendencies have increased, as the Berlin Conference of European Communist Parties in 1977 revealed. The debate over the issues raised, apart from driving a wedge between the ruling parties of Eastern Europe and the three most important parties in Western Europe, has split the British, Greek and Swedish parties among others.

Seen over a period of a hundred years the natural condition of European communism and socialism has therefore never been one of monolithic unity; and there is no inherent reason why such unity should prevail today, still less under the direction of Moscow. But during the three decades or so between the formation of the Comintern in 1919 and the death of Stalin in 1953 the natural diversity of European communism was held in check within an international communist movement controlled by the CPSU. During this period, first the Comintern and later the Cominform dictated party tactics and acted as an instrument of Soviet foreign policy. In particular, united or popular front tactics were invariably advocated when Moscow sought to co-operate with the West; and denounced when the Soviet Union retired into its shell. This is why between 1919 and 1953 European communism repeatedly oscillated between support for, and opposition to, alliance with non-communist parties.

In the early 1920s, the Comintern advocated united front tactics between communist and social democrat parties, while Lenin was pursuing his New Economic Policy and seeking trade and economic assistance from the West. At the end of the decade Stalin reversed the policy, denouncing social democrats as 'social fascists' while at home embarking on collectivisation and autarky. In 1935 Stalin introduced popular front tactics in the Comintern as a means of opposing fascism in Western Europe and mending his fences with Western Governments in the face of the Nazi threat. From 1939 to 1941, the period of the Nazi-Soviet Pact, this policy was thrown into reverse: as a result some Western European communist attitudes to Hitler were shamefully ambiguous. Between 1944 and 1946, when Stalin's main aim was to preserve the wartime alliance with the West, communist parties were once again encouraged to co-operate closely with non-communists. This led to PCF and PCI participation in government in the immediate post-war years. Although in France and Italy the communists were, because of their leading role in the Resistance, better placed than they had been before (and have been since) to seize power, Moscow enjoined moderation. This went as far as influencing the communist deputies in the Italian Constituent Assembly to vote for the Lateran Pacts which Mussolini had concluded with the Vatican and which guaranteed a continuing and influential role for the church in post-war Italian society and political life. At the same time, to minimise hostility to newly imposed communist Governments in Eastern Europe, Stalin was talking of the validity of distinct national roads to socialism.

Things changed yet again in 1947 with the onset of the Cold War. Unredeemed Stalinism—which played the role of both cause and effect in relation to the tensions of those years—dominated Eastern Europe and the international communist movement. The dangerous polarisation of hostility between East and West made it impossible for communist parties in Western Europe to participate in Government. With the establishment of the Cominform, Stalin returned popular front tactics to the shelf and the PCI and the PCF went into opposition.

Stalin's death in 1953 was in every way a major turning point: for the Soviet Union, for Eastern Europe, for the international communist movement and for East-West relations. When at the Twentieth Party Congress in 1956 Khrushchev denounced Stalinism, he triggered off a process which in the following twenty years progressively undermined the monolithic unity of communism in Europe and the world. The de-Stalinisation campaign and the damage this did to the moral authority of the Soviet Communist Party and the Cominform; the armed insurrection in Hungary and the riots in Poland in 1956; the split with China and the rival ideological centre which this created; the invasion of Czechoslovakia in 1968; the spread of marxist-orientated regimes in the Third World—all these things gave additional impetus to the centrifugal tendencies which the death of Stalin had released.

At the same time, Khrushchev's decision to abandon Stalin's doctrine of the inevitability of war with the capitalist world opened the way to Soviet policies of detente and peaceful co-existence. These policies once again made alliances with non-communists respectable. But by giving Western European communist parties room to manoeuvre between East and West, detente itself has proved to be a major centrifugal force within European communism.

In *Italy* the communist idea of a national road to socialism, based on a strategy of broad alliances with Catholic and non-communist interests, was a central feature in the thinking of the party's founder, Gramsci. When the Italian Communist Party was in Government between 1944 and 1947, it advocated a 'Pact of common action' with the Christian democrats and socialists as a basis for post-war reconstruction. In 1948, at its Sixth Party Congress, Togliatti coined the phrase 'the Italian road to socialism' to describe a policy of seeking power by peaceful and parliamentary means. In 1956, at the Eighth Party Congress, 'polycentrism' was officially endorsed while the plurality of parties under socialism was explicitly accepted. From then on, by way of Togliatti's Yalta Memorandum, published after his death in 1964, and Sig. Berlinguer's launching of the 'historic compromise' in 1973, Gramsci's original idea of a communist alliance with the other popular forces of Italian society was progressively refined and adapted to the conditions arising from de-Stalinisation and the emergence of detente. In 1963 the party had made its first major gesture of defiance towards Moscow when it opposed an inter-party conference to condemn the Chinese. Five years later the PCI condemned the Soviet invasion of Czechoslovakia.

This process took place against a background of growing polarisation between the Christian democrats and the communists. When the Communist Party left the Italian Government in 1947, it had slightly less than one-fifth of the national vote, the socialists slightly more. During 1947–8, the socialists split into two parties—the PSI and the PSDI—on the issue of co-operation with the communists. With the exception of a brief period of attempted reunion in 1968, the socialists have remained divided ever since. The result has been the progressive development of the PCI as the main alternative to Christian democracy. Since 1947, the Italian communists have steadily increased their share of the popular vote, reaching an all-time high of over 34 per cent in last year's general election. The comparable figures for the PSI and PSDI were 9·6 per cent and 3·4 per cent respectively.

In *France*, in sharp contrast to both Italy and Spain, the impact of de-Stalinisation took far longer to make itself felt. It was not until 1964 that the French Communist Party endorsed the return to a popular front strategy. Only in the last two years has the PCF taken an independent line and admitted in public to differences of view with Moscow. While the French party had condemned the Soviet invasion of Czechoslovakia in 1968, they subsequently gave their formal support to the programme of so-called normalisation which followed. In part, the reason is historical: although Maurice Thorez had spoken of a distinct French way to socialism in the 1930s and 1940s, there was no coherent intellectual base comparable to Gramsci's legacy to the PCI on which to build a French equivalent of the 'historic compromise'. More important, the concrete realities of post-war French politics have borne no resemblance to the situation in Italy.

For the last thirty years, the French Communist Party has had to compete on the left with the vigorous tradition of French socialism. The PCF has followed a trajectory opposite to that of its Italian counterpart in seeing its share of the national vote decline from about one-third to about one-fifth. In 1946, with their close identification with the Resistance still fresh in the minds of French voters, the communists gained almost 29 per cent of the popular vote with the socialists holding some 5 per cent less. In 1947, the PCF went into opposition, where again, unlike its Italian opposite number, the French party played a largely obstructive role. This, combined with the anti-communist sentiment of the majority of the French electorate during the Cold War, began to diminish its popularity. The socialists were for their part unable to take advantage of the situation. They found themselves submerged in predominantly conservative governing coalitions and, like most of the parties which made up the coalition Governments of the Fourth Republic, they frequently split on individual issues.

The return of General de Gaulle in 1958 transformed the situation. The Fifth Republic polarised political activity between the majority who supported de Gaulle and the left. Around whom was the left to organise its opposition to the Gaullist majority? In the 1960s, socialist attempts under M. Defferre to form a centre-left grouping failed. By contrast, M. Mitterrand believed that if the socialist party was to mount an effective challenge and, at the same time, compete effectively with the PCF, it would have to accept a communist alliance. In 1965, the communists supported M. Mitterrand in the presidential elections, helping him gain 45 per cent of the popular vote. In 1967, the socialists and communists formed an alliance for the general election which brought both of them substantial increases in the number of their seats in the National Assembly, with the PCF still maintaining a small percentage lead over the socialists. In 1973, the PCF and a radically reformed socialist party under M. Mitterrand fought the general election on the basis of a common programme of government, otherwise known as the Union of the Left. Between them the two parties, together with the left radicals, polled over 40 per cent of the vote with the socialists almost level-pegging with the communists at 20 per cent. In the following year, the Union of the Left almost brought M. Mitterrand to the presidency of France, but it failed to make him Prime Minister in March 1978.

The Union of the Left brought the Communist Party within striking distance of ministerial office. But it has also sharpened the struggle for power on the left by increasing the strength of the French socialists. It is too soon to say whether the Union of the Left is beyond repair, following the rift between the communists and socialists in September 1977 and the disappointing election results in March 1978. Nor can one speak with certainty about the motives which led the communists to precipitate that rift. But it seems that a major element in their calculation was concern to assert their influence within the left if they were not to pay too high a price for a possible place in Government.

In *Spain*, the Communist Party has only just emerged from forty years' illegality. But as early as 1956 the party was advocating a policy of so-called national reconciliation for the post-Franco era based on broad political alliances. During the 1960s the party co-operated with left-wing Catholic groups in underground trade union activity and made repeated overtures to other opposition groups. A major rift occurred with the Soviet Union in 1968 when Sñr Carrillo denounced the invasion of Czechoslovakia. In the early 1970s relations with the Soviet Union worsened when Moscow supported a pro-Soviet splinter group. The party's present demand for a broad-based coalition Government, including communists, not only follows established policy, but is a logical reaction to a situation in which at the last count the party had only about 9 per cent of the national vote and the radical Spanish Workers Socialist Party about 24 per cent.

The line of development since 1945 of the communist parties of France, Italy and Spain, and in particular their response to changing international conditions after Stalin's death, has therefore been far from uniform. But by the mid-1970s, their separate national roads had brought them to broadly similar conclusions about the best means of achieving power.

Western European communist parties run a constant risk of being forced to choose between cultivating their wider bourgeois constituency and maintaining their traditional role as the vanguard party of the working class. The continued pursuit of electoral success means constantly consolidating the gains made outside the working class and, if possible, extending them into further layers of the bourgeoisie: in a recent lecture in London Sñr Carrillo said that his aim was to draw votes from the centre and right of the Spanish political spectrum. But the wider their social base, the greater the internal and policy contradictions and the danger of schism. There have already been rumblings of working-class discontent because the PCI and PCE support the packages of economic reforms which the Italian and Spanish Governments respectively have introduced and in which wage restraint plays a major part.

The communists are therefore vulnerable to outflanking movements within the left. In France and Spain the danger is acute since the PCF and PCE are competing for the same constituency as radical and electorally stronger socialist parties who have no need constantly to prove their democratic credentials through gestures of moderation. In both countries, the communist parties have been accused of conservatism by the socialists. In France there is the additional risk that within the Union of the Left the PCF will lose its identity to an electorally stronger party. Tensions of this kind have provoked a crisis in the alliance between the communists and socialists. In Italy, where the socialist parties are weaker than the PCI, this problem does not arise, though the PCI faces a challenge from the ultra-left among students and workers.

By associating themselves, whether or not in formal coalition, with Government policies which prove unpopular or unsuccessful, especially on economic and social matters, the communists risk electoral disaster. The PCI, by co-operating in a programme with a minority Christian democrat administration, is open to the accusation by elements within the party of accepting responsibility without power and thus losing the sympathy of its electoral base. At the same time it is argued that a decision to withdraw support from the Government and thus precipitate a major political and economic crisis would destroy the party's carefully cultivated image of responsibility and moderation and prejudice its entire strategy of achieving a lasting alliance with the other main popular forces in Italy.

Participation in successful Governments will not necessarily be advantageous if the result is to strengthen the other partners in the coalition. In Italy it is still an open question whether the Christian democrats might not derive as much or more electoral advantage from a successful coalition with the PCI as the PCI could hope to do. Both the Socialist and the Republican

Parties in Italy have suffered electorally from their co-operation with Christian democrats in the past; and it is not inconceivable that the PCI, despite its relatively much stronger electoral position, could suffer in the same way.

For the Soviet Union it might seem that communist participation in Governments in Europe would be tangible evidence of the advance of the 'forces of the left'. Such an advance of the 'forces of the left' would tend also to support the Soviet contention that, in the words of a Politburo candidate member in 1974, there has recently been 'a qualitative shift in the crisis of capitalism' with recession, unemployment and inflation hitting the Western democracies. The Russians might be expected to regard the advance of the left as one of the main political bonuses of detente, which should lead to an enhancement of their influence in Europe. But as communism in Europe has adapted to the political style and mood of each country, so a number of dilemmas and direct challenges to the Soviet Union have created a paradoxical situation. The so-called crisis of capitalism of the 1970s has coincided with something coming very near to a crisis of communism.

The Soviet Union, in deciding its response, faces its long-standing problem of reconciling state and party interests. In the days of the Comintern and Cominform the Soviet Union was able to reconcile these differences on its own terms. This is no longer possible. The Soviet Union as the self-proclaimed leader of the world communist movement has an obligation to support Western European communist parties. But the various communist parties pose a complicating factor for Soviet inter-state relations and this at a time when detente is the central plank of Soviet foreign policy. The French and Italian Communist Parties have become politically so strong on a national level that the Soviet Union must deal with them not only as fraternal parties but also as political forces in their own right, influencing Government policies and therefore inter-state relations. Furthermore, the entry of a communist party into the Government of a major Western power could upset the delicate equilibrium on which detente rests and so provoke instability in East-West relations.

Communism in Western Europe presents a triple challenge

to the authority of the CPSU: in the world communist movement, in Eastern Europe and in the Soviet Union itself. The Soviet position is that the theory, experience and practice of the Soviet party are the main guarantee of success in the struggle against capitalism. National peculiarities may be taken into account in determining paths for socialism, but the true marxist-leninist cannot depart from basic revolutionary principles of which the CPSU is the chief repository. These principles are brought together in two concepts, the 'dictatorship of the proletariat' and 'proletarian internationalism', both of which have been dropped by the parties of Italy, France and Spain.

The entry into Government in Western Europe of a communist party would give new prominence to revisionist marxism which could have dangerously destabilising repercussions on the regimes of Eastern Europe. Some of these regimes have displayed a marked ambiguity towards their Western comrades and in particular to the emphasis on independent national roads to socialism.

Although all of the Western communist parties are strong supporters of detente, because its continuation is an indispensable condition for their entire political strategy, there is an apparent divergence between some of their professed foreign policy goals and those of the Soviet Union. The PCI and PCE profess support for the European Community and the idea of European political unity. The Russians have publicly branded the Spanish party's ideas as an attempt to establish a European force 'opposed primarily to the Socialist States'. The PCF and PCI ostensibly give qualified support for their countries' continued membership of the Atlantic Alliance and profess to disavow the unilateral dismantling of NATO.

Although they fall far short of rupture with the Soviet Union, there can be no doubt about the reality of the differences which have arisen between Moscow and these three parties. What exactly this tells us about the nature of their commitment to pluralist democracy is another matter. For the democratic socialist, the central paradox remains: that a political phenomenon which draws its political support from the ballot-box could at the end of the day prove to be the instrument which closes the ballot-boxes for good.

All communists in Western Europe claim that their goal is to transform capitalist society. They readily admit that they differ fundamentally from social democrats. What evidence is there to support their assertion that pluralist values will survive the transformation from capitalist to communist societies?

The blunt fact is there is no evidence. This is not an issue on which one can afford to compromise. In the 1940s communist leaders in Eastern Europe made similar commitments to pluralist democracy, none of which was honoured. (Though it is argued—and with some justice—that Eastern Europe's strategic importance to the Soviet Union, its level of economic and social development, and the Cold War atmosphere of thirty years ago do not provide accurate analogies with the situations today in Italy, France and Spain.)

In Italy, the PCI has administered the region of Emilia-Romagna for thirty years. But the communists' apparently democratic behaviour in regional government gives no conclusive evidence of how they would behave in a central Government which they dominated.

The plain truth is that open support for the ballot-box is the only feasible path to political power for all Western communist parties. The espousal of the ballot-box is a political necessity for them. The explanation for their conversion is power. You have to search hard for any underlying philosophical justification for democracy, any espousal of libertarian values, any fundamental respect for diversity, any political humility. Professions of support for pluralist democracy give us no guarantees of how political power, once acquired, would be used. In particular, the vagueness with which the parties describe the situation following the transition to communism can only increase suspicions. As Sñr Carrillo was quoted as saying in 1974: 'All we can say on this subject belongs to the sphere of future prospects as we see them, without it being possible to rely on precedents.'

The central difficulty in resolving these questions is that by any calculation, including that of individual communists, the 'building of socialism', as they call it, must be a long-term process and definitive answers will have to await its conclusion. Sñr Carrillo has said that socialism cannot be hurried. Sig.

Berlinguer has made the point that even with 51 per cent of the popular vote—and only the PCI is remotely within striking distance of such a figure—the Italian Communist Party would not be able on its own to introduce the kind of reforms which it considers necessary to transform Italian society. The spectre of Chile—of what happened when Allende's Government, democratically elected though by a minority of the popular vote, tried to force a country with powerful bourgeois institutions on to a socialist path—has had an indelible impact on all three parties. Their leaders are fully aware, in the words of Isaac Deutscher, that to provoke a counter-revolutionary reaction a revolution 'need do no more than cast a shadow'.

What we must do to try and resolve some of these questions is challenge communists in each and every Western European country to be open and specific about the central issues. In particular, we must focus attention and demand answers on what remains a fundamental difference between democratic socialists and communists: party tactics and internal party organisation.

Democracy, like charity, begins at home. We have therefore the right to ask if there is not a glaring discrepancy between the pluralist professions of all these Western communist parties and their continuing attachment to the principles of 'democratic centralism' in their internal organisation. In what way is the monolithic, vertical structure of the three main 'Eurocommunist' parties any different from the ruling parties of Eastern Europe and the Soviet Union? Party discipline is one thing, but what kind of discipline is it that, in the case of the French party, could from one day to the next switch from unanimous opposition to unanimous support for the French nuclear deterrent? It is understandable that in Franco's Spain the Communist Party could not survive without a clandestine cell system and could influence state institutions only by infiltrating them. But in free and open societies what possible democratic justification can there be for clandestine infiltration and political cells? Why do the parties refuse to admit to internal divisions like any other? Why is it necessary for decisions always to be accepted unanimously? The pursuit of a false consensus leads inevitably to the secrecy of party proceedings; to the stifling of open debate and criticism of party policies and leaders; to nominated lists in internal elections; and to purges of dissident party members. All these things are objectionable to democratic socialists and all are practised to a lesser or greater degree by communist parties in Western Europe.

We must also ask for a more precise and detailed explanation of how the pluralist commitment will be honoured once socialism has arrived. Would a party system still operate? If not, how would the essential requirement — the plurality of opinions — be guaranteed and articulated? Sñr Carrillo has said that a communist party must be able to resign from Government in good time if it does not have the support of the majority of the people. Yet some communists do not seem to be able to envisage this as a practical possibility. One member of the Italian communist leadership, Sig. Radice, has said: 'Would any part of the population want to see a regression from socialism, a retreat from a higher to a lower form of society? ... It is entirely unhistorical as well as unreasonable to suppose that they would want to turn the clock back.'

A further crucial test will be for the parties to maintain their independent line and commitment to parliamentary democracy in the face of electoral set-backs. In Italy, it has been no accident that the policy of 'historic compromise' has been adopted by the PCI during a period of constant electoral success. In France, are we by contrast witnessing in the disintegration of the Union of the Left a reversal of the Communist Party's parliamentary strategy under pressure of a weakening electoral position in relation to the socialists? If, as the parties maintain, communism is a long-term strategy, it must be able to withstand the ups and downs of electoral fortune.

These are some of the fundamental questions which the development of communism in Western Europe raises for democratic socialists. It is, however, no use looking on this development as an alien organism, to be treated contemptuously. It is a very serious phenomenon which needs analysis and debate. It is an indigenous product of national political processes and of a widely felt need for change and, for millions of Europeans, it has provided the means of re-engaging in the democratic process. The effectiveness of the communist

Resistance in occupied France or fascist Spain, or of efficient local government by communists in Italy, have all provided the communist parties in these countries with a degree of support that is itself an indictment of the failure of democratic socialist parties to produce and implement effective policies. Yet, at the same time, it is the very broadness of the spectrum to which the communists are appealing in these countries which gives hope to democratic socialists. Democratic socialism can and should win back those voters.

Deliberately in analysing the three strongest communist parties in Western Europe the term 'Eurocommunism' has not been discussed. There are grounds for deep scepticism that any such unified phenomenon exists. It is a dangerous term. It confers a coherence and a respectability on an ill-defined, disparate and as yet unidentifiable phenomenon. It is very interesting that Western communist leaders themselves are now using the word 'Eurocommunism'. They recognise it has an appealing quality. It is a convenient portmanteau term. It tends to make people suspend their critical faculties, avoid analysing the phenomenon seriously, country by country, and instead take refuge in 'generalities. 'Eurocommunism' is becoming respectable. It is a term which socialists should eschew. It should be given no currency. We should reject it unless convinced that the phenomenon which it is supposed to describe exists as a separate entity. In rejecting the term one is refusing to accept that communism anywhere, particularly in Europe, is a coherent entity. Rejecting the vocabulary makes it easier to prevent any lowering of the guard of democratic socialists. We should rebut any attempt to link the British Communist Party with 'Eurocommunism', any attempt to persuade the Labour Party to confer on British communists the same credibility as some would wish to give to their Italian, French and Spanish counterparts.

The Labour Party must not be turned away from its present outright opposition and traditional hostility to the Communist Party in Britain. We must resist all blandishments to tolerate, then to associate and then to combine with the communists under the broad banner of the left and embrace within the heady froths of 'Eurocommunism'. We must resist, for it would not only spell electoral death for the Labour Party but it would weaken the most effective mass movement against communism in Western Europe and indeed in the world.

Instead, we in Britain should approach French communism in relation first to how French socialists wish us to approach French communists. The British Labour Party's prime relationship is with our fellow French socialists or Italian socialists or Spanish socialists. This was the wise approach adopted when the Labour Party considered inviting delegations from communist parties to its Annual Conference. We first consulted, and only proceeded if we had the agreement of, the relevant socialist party. In working with our fellow socialists we are bound to pay due regard to their own national political circumstances and their own national involvement with their communist parties. But it is not part of our philosophy to work independently with their communist parties. We should deliberately fragment so-called 'Eurocommunism' so as to deal with it country by country, recognising that vigilance should be our watch-word and that it is not in the interest of democratic socialism to promote communism at the expense of our fellow socialists anywhere in Europe.

Most writings and speeches in the West on so-called 'Eurocommunism' start by talking about the threat which it poses, the dangers to NATO, the difficulties for the EEC. There are dangers in starting from that point. Although one cannot ignore this factor, not only do threats solidify support but there are institutional problems. The real battle is for people's minds. Communism in Western Europe presents a long-term challenge to our democratic society rather than an immediate threat to our institutions. Its appeal is built on dissatisfaction with existing European political parties, the failure to tackle serious defects in our society, high unemployment, gross inequalities of wealth and power, and even, in Italy, the issue of law and order. Evoking fear, implying that we will not accept them as partners in NATO and the EEC if they win elections in their countries is the worst possible response. It undermines our own commitment to accepting the verdict of the ballot-box. There are good reasons for thinking that the leaders of the differing Western communist parties themselves do not want, in the midst of a world recession, to be propelled into the difficult, direct responsibilities of Government. We will not be able to combat communism without first attempting an examination of the nature of communism in Europe and analysing its weaknesses, particularly its democratic basis. The challenge to democratic socialism is to rediscover its own radicalism, to attract back into its fold the young and disillusioned, and to strengthen our own international links. The challenge is an extremely serious one. It is a challenge to democrats in general but to democratic socialists in particular. As the French socialist Léon Blum observed: 'Without socialism democracy is imperfect; without democracy socialism is helpless.'

5

Race Relations in Britain

At the tail end of our imperial history Britain is faced with a particularly difficult and intractable problem called 'race', a crude euphemism for the debate about the future role in our society of black and brown immigrants from the Commonwealth and their descendants.

It flows directly from the decision of the post-war Labour Government to pull out of the colonies and to replace Empire with Commonwealth and create a Commonwealth citizenship. It is a problem which is exceptionally complex and which arouses deep emotions. Yet unless it is solved fairly and justly our colonial record, on balance a good one, and Britain's voice as a source of moral and political leadership in the world, will be hopelessly diminished.

It is an issue where our theoretical liberalism of the 1950s and 1960s is being tested against the harsh and fundamentally different reality of the late 1970s. The history of Commonwealth immigration into our country demonstrates that few topics are so complex. It calls for cool and responsible leadership. Yet simple and emotive slogans too often hold sway.

It is not a politician's duty to articulate and play upon people's gut feelings, nor to use opinion polls to detect and measure popular prejudices, and then with skilled public relations techniques to articulate those prejudices. On race, the politician needs to do more than exploit the lowest common denominator of mass emotion.

The dangers of racialism need no emphasising. There is no 'solution' to racialism except to reject it and to combat it implacably. At Yad Vashem on the Mount of Memory in West Jerusalem is a museum set up in 1953 to perpetuate the memory

73

of the six million Jewish victims of the Nazi holocaust. It is a vivid and poignant reminder of the consequences of Adolf Hitler's 'final solution' to the 'Jewish problem'. At Yad Vashem, as Leon Felipe wrote, 'Israel holds the largest collection of the world's tears.' Yet racialism—whether taken to its full conclusion in the unspeakable evils of Dachau and Belsen or whether at the kindergarten stage as in the case of the National Front and its thugs in Britain—is always vicious and destructive. At home we do not always recognise racialism when we see it. People abroad take a more critical view of the British, and matters which sometimes seem to us to be of passing journalistic or political significance can be picked up in Africa, the Middle East or the Caribbean and are there seen in a different light. Racialist outbursts, whether against black or brown immigrants or Jewish people in Britain or in favour of racist regimes abroad, tarnish our image and inhibit our capacity to play a full part in world affairs.

The present immigration controversy in Britain is not new. Jewish immigration, in particular into London during the period 1880 to 1910, provoked very similar reactions. It is remarkable how similar the language and vocabulary of the debate about immigration at that time was to some of the language used today. The Ashkenazy Jews who came at the end of the last century were often perceived as a threat not only to the host society but also to the established Jewish community. Propagandists argued that this group was ideologically and culturally so sharply distinct as to be culturally unassimilable. And even the TUC, in 1892, 1894 and 1895 passed resolutions deploring the 'wholesale importation of Jewish alien workers'. As today, the racialist clichés were confused and contradictory; the immigrants were said to be hard workers who took Englishmen's jobs, yet they were also seen as lazy spongers.

It is nearly thirty years since the British Nationality Act of 1948 came into force. It created a citizenship to be held by those connected with Britain and with the large number of colonies then still in existence. All such citizens—as well as the citizens of the independent Commonwealth countries—continued to have the right of free entry to Britain until it was first found necessary fourteen years later to impose restrictions. This was the idealistic principle of *civis britannicus sum*, and, in the days before full employment and wider knowledge of the English language, caused no problems. In post-war Britain there were many more jobs than native Britons to do them. As migrants from the Commonwealth and colonies began to arrive in a haphazard fashion, the Government was also accepting refugees from the displaced persons' camps of Europe. Our idealism about Commonwealth citizenship and the needs of our domestic labour market still coincided at that time. Subsequently— usually with reluctance and often in haste—successive Governments introduced a series of Commonwealth immigration controls. Now, effectively, Commonwealth citizens are no freer to enter this country than aliens. The Immigration Act of 1971 completely replaced both the Commonwealth Immigrants Acts of 1962 and 1968 (and the Immigration Appeals Act of 1969) and the old and very different aliens legislation and the Aliens Order made under it. Broadly its effect is that all non-belongers —whether citizens of the UK and colonies lacking close ties with the UK itself, or other Commonwealth citizens, or foreign nationals—are now subject to the same basic immigration controls. Nationals of member countries of the EEC, and certain Commonwealth citizens (those with ancestral ties, and those settled before 1973 and their dependants) have a special position.

Now, within a framework of extremely tight immigration controls, there are demands that the commitments which remain—commitments acknowledged by the Conservative Government when they introduced the 1971 Act—should be dishonoured. It would be morally and politically wrong to dishonour those commitments. The British people, if offered rational explanations and sensible arguments rather than over-simple and emotive slogans, will understand what racialism is and why it should be implacably opposed.

Immigrants did not come here because Governments were negligent or stupid. Many came because they were invited, while others came to flee unemployment at home and to take jobs here. Mr E. J. B. Rose in his book *Colour and Citizenship* has shown how closely the arrival in Britain of black and brown immigrants from the Commonwealth is bound up with the recent history of our economy and our society.* Mr Rose describes Commonwealth immigration as a 'tracer element' which—as it passes through society—shows up like an X-ray the employment structure of our society since the war, the state of our cities and the housing market, the relative status of jobs and the importance we have given to certain essential social services.

It is frequently forgotten that Commonwealth immigrants came to Britain, in the main, at a time of acute labour shortage. To this day immigrants are not found in those parts of the country where there is acute unemployment, such as Northern Ireland, most of Scotland and Wales, the North East of England or the West Country. Immigrants came in the 1940s, 1950s and 1960s to the more prosperous parts of the country—to the places where there were jobs. But that is not the whole story. In these regions immigrants came to the inner city areas, to the declining urban centres to do jobs which the native population on the whole preferred not to do.

Commonwealth immigration is therefore tightly bound up with changes in the pattern of life of working people in this country. Until, roughly speaking, before the Second World War, most ordinary working people lived in city centres. They lived in densely populated areas, often in old Edwardian or Victorian tenements or terraces, and they moved within a narrow circle, usually going to work or to visit friends on foot. Since the 1920s and 1930s, and particularly during the period following the Second World War, car-owning expanded from the middle class to the working class, employment patterns altered and many of the more prosperous people moved from the inner city to the new outer suburbs, either taking advantage of the boom in council-house building which took place under the post-war Labour Government or else moving to new private estates in the suburbs or even into country areas. The post-war history of inner London boroughs such as Islington, Lambeth and Wandsworth is one of outward migration by the prosperous white worker, and inward migration by Irish and Commonwealth immigrants, while, conversely, outer London boroughs

* *Colour and Citizenship : Report on British Race Relations* (Oxford University Press, 1969).

such as Croydon or Barnet have seen an enormous growth in their population and an expansion of their services and amenities. The old, the less skilled and the newcomers have stayed in decaying inner cities, while the successful and more prosperous have moved to newer outer areas.

The old Victorian houses, the old schools and the old hospital buildings have become gradually less and less appropriate to the needs of modern society. Alongside the white population which has tended in the inner city to consist disproportionately of those least able to cope with society, immigrants, often with language and other social difficulties, have moved in. We therefore have the paradox that while the successful in our society have been able to move to new and expanded areas on the outskirts of our cities, the poor, the old and the newcomers have been living alongside each other in areas where the social structure has been increasingly inadequate or deficient.

Commonwealth immigrants arrived in Britain, then, not as tourists or merchants, but as workers, and they entered British society at the bottom. They came to the most prosperous parts of the country, but, within them, moved to the declining districts. They entered those jobs which were being vacated by a suburbanising native population and came into those areas which were themselves declining in popularity and where cheap and often poor-quality housing was more or less freely available. The Commonwealth immigrant population managed to find places to live in the decaying areas of British cities and functioned as a supplementary work force. Some of the first jobs the West Indians came to do, for example, were in transport. The Barbados recruiting offices of London Transport opened in 1955 and were responsible until 1970 for the recruitment of approximately 4,000 London Transport workers. Many others came freely without a work contract. The immigration of Commonwealth workers during the 1950s shows a peak of 47,000 in 1956, when there were nearly a million job vacancies, but goes down to 21,000 in 1959 when there were 650,000 job vacancies. By the early 1960s when the children who were born as part of the post-war 'bulge', when families were reunited after the war, began to appear on the labour market, the first measures to control and ultimately stop Commonwealth immigration were being introduced.

It is necessary to study the migration statistics. Interestingly enough, Britain is a net exporter of people; between 1971 and 1976 there was a net loss to this country of 219,000. And recently very few new immigrants have come in as workers. The families of the workers have tended to enter some time after the breadwinner or family head. Thus, West Indian workers came in large numbers in the late 1950s and early 1960s, and by 1967 the influx of dependants of West Indian workers began to tail off sharply. In the case of Asians, the peak of the workers was not reached until 1963 and, as a result, the peak of Asian dependants was not reached until the late 1960s, with the Pakistan high of 17,506 dependants being reached in 1967. Now the immigration of West Indians to this country is almost complete. Indeed, in recent years more West Indians have emigrated than have come in; they have either returned to the West Indies or re-emigrated to other countries such as the United States or Canada. In the case of the Indians, Pakistanis and Bangladeshis the process of entry by close dependants of people already settled here is not yet complete. We have a commitment to the wives and children, and our rules also cover the entry of fiancé(e)s of either sex, and certain other close dependants in tightly defined categories where the claim is essentially compassionate, as in the case of widowed mothers and elderly and dependent parents. But the number of new heads of household admitted with work permits for employment in now minuscule.

The number of new work permit holders from the New Commonwealth and Pakistan will remain tiny (1,735 in 1976, 1,317 in 1977—figures which include those with only short-term or trainee work permits), while the number of dependants will continue to decrease over the next few years. The number of immigrants from the New Commonwealth and Pakistan accepted for settlement in 1977 was 44,155, 20 per cent fewer than in 1976 when the figure was 55,013.

We should realise that no political party in this country has a monopoly of common sense or of folly on the subject of immigration. It was a Conservative Government and a Conservative

Home Secretary, Mr Robert Carr, who in the summer of 1972 coped honourably with the challenge to community relations in this country which was posed by the expulsion by President Amin of Uganda of the entire Asian community in his country, including at the time at least 40,000 citizens of the UK and Colonies. While in some localities the atmosphere did turn sour many organisations and individuals came forward to help with the resettlement process. Race had never become a party issue until recently. Many people from all parties struggled to maintain the right of free entry for Commonwealth citizens. When, in the early 1960s, the then Conservative Government introduced the first Commonwealth Immigrants Bill, prominent Conservatives stated that it would be 'tragic' to end the right of free entry; while the Labour Party bitterly opposed the introduction of Commonwealth immigration controls and did not accept the need for them until some time after the Wilson Government was elected in 1964. Today, many people still feel uneasy about the need for immigration controls as such, probably because the open door policy was for so long accepted bi-partisan policy in this country, and also because immigration control has often been claimed to be racialist in itself. Britain, like any other country, needs a sensible and well-administered immigration policy, but it would be unacceptable for immigration control to be administered on a racial basis.

One of the most striking features of the 'numbers game' is the way we generalise with emotive judgments; numbers are bandied about in isolation and not set within a disciplined framework of rational judgment. For example, the number of dependants coming in at the moment, something like 30,000 a year, is said to be 'too high', but no one has attempted to establish why this figure is too high, or why 15,000 might be acceptable; or what figure would be acceptable. Immigration should be viewed, together with natural increase, death and emigration, as only one of several factors affecting the structure of our population. It is on fears and uncertainties that racialism feeds, and vague and emotive phrases and meaningless statistics feed those fears.

In moving away from sterile talk about immigration statistics, we have to realise that to cope with the problem of race relations there are two distinct and separate errors of policy which need tackling. There is first the actual racial dimension—the misunderstandings or frictions that can arise because people of different backgrounds, cultures and races live together. This includes the problem of racialism in general, but it also involves education of all sections of the community about living together, and it involves in particular giving information to immigrants about life in Britain. It means assisting immigrant children to learn English and to adapt to our society. This is a difficult and delicate area of policy. The second area of importance to race relations is more manageable, but still requires vision and energy. This wider area is what is called 'inner city policy'— in other words, tackling the deprivation and poor conditions which are now typical of many of our city centres but which are by no means peculiar to immigrants.

On the question of community relations, the Race Relations Act of 1966 which was followed by a further Act in 1968 and ultimately taken over by the Race Relations Act of 1976, were the first attempts by Government to tackle by legislation the problem of racial discrimination and community relations. The 1976 Act set up the Commission for Racial Equality, which, in addition to its role as an educator of minority groups and of public opinion, has the task of supervising the anti-discrimination legislation and indeed of initiating legal action where it thinks fit. In tackling specific areas of our national life where racial discrimination still exists—in, for example, house sales or in employment—this Act, and the work of the Commission, are of crucial importance.

The 1968 Act reorganised on a statutory basis the Community Relations Councils, which had been set up previously as voluntary liaison committees in areas of resettlement to bring together members of the immigrant and native communities to discuss matters of mutual concern and to seek common solutions to common problems. Most towns and cities with a large immigrant population now have a Community Relations Council and at least one Community Relations Officer. Their work often only reaches the press when sensational issues arise, although in fact a great deal of low-key constructive work assisting communities to integrate the immigrants has gone on under the aegis of local Community Relations Councils. Teachers, doctors, social workers and other key members of the community have been brought face-to-face with the immigrant communities; while the immigrant leaders have been able to make direct contact with the leaders of local authorities and of local political and other organisations to discuss their people's problems.

Although disadvantage is not something which only racial minorities suffer from, we have recognised that there are special disadvantages arising particularly from language and cultural differences and unfamiliarity with the country. It is important that, in addition to the massive increase in the urban programme, eligible local authorities should make use of the special funds available under Section II of the Local Government Act of 1966 to assist with the cost of staff specially provided in consequence of the presence within their areas of immigrants from the Commonwealth whose language or customs differ from those of the indigenous community. Expenditure eligible for this grant during the year 1977–8 was estimated at about £28 million. The bulk of the grant goes to help provide additional teachers in primary and secondary schools but it also assists with the salaries of liaison officers, interpreters, social workers, those looking after children in care and in day nurseries, and environmental health officers.

The Labour Government set up the Centre for the Study of Disadvantage in Manchester, to establish where the educational needs of the disadvantaged, including immigrant children, lie and to spread good practice among teachers. The Department of the Environment and the Home Office are conducting research to identify the origins of strain and stress in housing and to establish what measures can be taken to ensure a fairer distribution of housing resources. In the field of employment, a sustained effort is being made to monitor the progress of immigrants and coloured workers. For the sake of good race relations, we need to monitor what is happening to the longer-standing immigrants from the New Commonwealth and their children.

In Britain there are many more poor white people than poor blacks and browns. But, in proportion to their total numbers, more of the blacks and browns are poor. And many of them live in the inner areas of our towns and cities, where they suffer not only from specific racial disadvantage, but from the general deprivation which affects all those who live there. The White Paper 'Policy for the Inner Cities', published in June 1977, recognised that while towns and cities of all sizes have problems of decline, they are most marked in parts of our major cities, where school buildings and hospitals are often inadequate and there is difficulty in attracting suitable professional people to man some essential services. The Government is now taking major steps to tackle the problems of our inner cities. The existing Urban Programme of under £30 million a year is to be increased to £125 million during 1979–80. Not all the areas contain large ethnic minority populations but where they are present, they often have the greatest needs, and they will be among those who will benefit from the measures we are taking. As the White Paper explains, the inner areas are being given a new priority in main policies and programmes. In addition, certain local authorities with severe physical, social and economic problems have been invited to draw up comprehensive programmes for their inner cities. In seven areas, where these problems are at their worst, the programmes will be drawn up by central and local government working in partnership. These programmes will be reinforced by funds from the Urban Programme, which is being increased and extended. However, assistance under the Urban Programme will remain available to all local authorities with areas of special social need. The Government has also legislated to give local authorities with serious inner area problems enhanced powers to assist industry. These measures are aimed at improving the inner city environment and its social structure and at bringing back employment opportunities. All Government Departments need to look at their expenditure programme with a view to ensuring greater selectivity in channelling resources on the basis of need. The Department of Health through the work of the Resource Allocation Working Party has shown how it is possible to allocate health resources to achieve greater social justice and to monitor progress.* Britain needs a Social Audit to focus attention on

* See *In Sickness and in Health: The Politics of Medicine* by David Owen (Quartet Books, 1976), Chapter 4.

expenditure. We have spent decades arguing about global levels of expenditure but have given too little attention to the monitoring of expenditure to ensure that it is actually being spent on the areas of greatest need.

We have an obligation to provide a high standard of family medical care in the inner city. Research shows the need for energetic measures to combat deprivation and disadvantage amongst immigrant children in London. Families whose routines and traditions are seriously disrupted when they emigrate to Britain, and who find great difficulty in absorbing and adapting to the new culture, frequently find themselves in the position of having less time for their children either than comparable English parents or than their fellow countrymen at home. It has been shown that West Indian children have demonstrably suffered from their parents' immigration into the poorer areas of our cities. West Indian children were rarely taken out by their parents, rarely had holidays, had fewer toys than English children and were experiencing a much lower standard of living even than English children of a comparable socio-economic background. The children surveyed in 1972 are now in secondary school. They started off with a massive disadvantage because of these cultural factors. One of the ways in which we can help these children is by recognising the desirability of linking the care, education and health services for the three- and four-year-olds in areas of educational and social disadvantage, and by encouraging local authorities planning an expansion of nursery education to ensure that it is available for those children who need it most.

Nothing is more important for future generations than that we use all the resources at our disposal. If we just respond with a general discussion of 'immigration', a term which arouses fears and emotions, we will only divert attention from the very real problems which need to be tackled. Without energetic measures to deal with youth unemployment in the inner city in general and youth unemployment among ethnic minorities in particular, we shall be ensuring that whole generations of our young people in the inner cities—many of whom are black and brown—start their adult life embittered and frustrated. The Annual Report of the ILEA Careers Service for 1976–7 stated that in Division 9 (the London Borough of Lambeth) the unemployment rate for black youngsters is two or three times greater than for white young people. This is an infinitely more alarming statistic than the projections of the future size of the coloured population. The Government has acted and the new Youth Opportunities Programme of the Manpower Services Commission (which came into force on 1 April 1978) is an unprecedented and energetic answer to the problem of youth unemployment.

These are testing times for those who believe that Britain should not only be a repository of civilised values itself but also project those values to the world at large. At home the social costs of the immigration of the workers who kept our economy going at a time of full employment are having to be paid at a time of economic depression. We can speak with no authority in the world if we appear to condone or connive at racialism at home. That is why we must accept the fact of our multi-racial society, resolve to gain from its diversity, and tackle positively in Britain what is only one facet of an increasingly multi-racial world.

6

Apartheid

Racialism exists in many parts of the world but it is in South Africa, where racialism has been institutionalised in the policy of apartheid, that the world faces its greatest challenge. Britain needs a coherent and sustainable policy towards South Africa which will last into the 1980s. We need a policy which can demonstrate to the world that our commitment against racialism is total and our championing of human rights universal. Our post-war record of decolonisation in Africa was broadly successful until, in 1965, Rhodesia made its illegal declaration of independence. Ever since then Britain has found itself at the centre of controversy in Southern African politics. Our repeated failure to resolve the Rhodesian problem and our obvious economic links with South Africa have led many African countries to doubt our commitment to majority rule and our attitude to race. To analyse our position we must first look back into history, for many of our current problems have their roots in the past.

The scramble for power in Africa by European countries such as France, Portugal, Belgium and Germany in the 1880s began to change the nature of colonisation. Throughout the nineteenth century Britain had been reluctant to assume colonial commitments beyond the minimum compatible with preserving its strategic interests: maintaining free trade and, where necessary, protecting our missionaries. Even when the era of imperialist rivalry was well under way, Britain still tried to avoid direct involvement and policed and administered its Empire with an extremely small number of British soldiers and administrators. The second Boer War, in which we invested almost 450,000 men and enormous sums of money, only confirmed us in our determination—rooted in our experience in Canada, Australia and in the War of American Independence—to encourage the self-reliance of the colonies and not to become involved in wars with the settlers.

The long-term consequences of this policy in Africa were both beneficial and highly damaging. On the one hand, there was no attempt, as in some colonial empires, to assimilate the African territories into the metropolitan power. Britain avoided the trauma of the last-ditch efforts after 1945 to maintain the fiction of integration with the metropolitan power experienced by other European countries, which meant not only long delays in granting independence to their territories, but also that these delays were frequently accompanied by bloody and damaging wars of independence. Algeria was one example, but more recently Mozambique and Angola have had to endure a bitter struggle to replace the metropolitan power. Whatever Britain's motives—and they were a mixture of idealism and enlightened self-interest—British encouragement of local self-reliance never presented us with the temptation of claiming, and trying to enforce the claim, that our African colonies were an organic part of the United Kingdom.

Yet the British policy of encouraging local self-rule led in both South Africa and Rhodesia, though the circumstances were very different, to the entrenchment of white minority interests and the evolution of racialist societies. History may judge this policy as being far more damaging in the long term because of the birth of institutionalised racialism.

In the early decades of the nineteenth century a more humanitarian attitude to the under-privileged, both at home and overseas, began to gain ground in Britain. In 1833, slavery was abolished throughout the Empire. In South Africa itself the work of the London Missionary Society did much to bring home to the British Government and British public opinion their duty to defend the human rights of the native peoples. In the 1830s, the Colonial Office acted to protect the non-Europeans and Bantu tribes and their lands in South Africa. Non-Europeans were brought under the protection of the law. Land which had been annexed by the authorities was returned to the Bantu tribes.

It was precisely these humanitarian policies which pushed the land-hungry Boers in 1836 beyond the Orange River on what has become known as the Great Trek. The direct result was the foundation of the independent Afrikaner Republics of the Transvaal and the Orange Free State where from the outset Afrikaner attitudes excluded any possibility of racial partnership with the black and coloured peoples.

Britain for her part gave Cape Colony internal self-government in 1872 on a non-racial, if highly limited, franchise. Even then it was the expectation that, if only for economic reasons, societies would evolve in the territories of Southern Africa in which whites and non-Europeans could live together in harmony.

But we did not pursue these relatively enlightened policies with either consistency or firmness. One consequence of the Great Trek was the progressive expropriation by the Afrikaner Republics of black African lands. Many of the wars fought with local tribes in the decades following the Great Trek were caused by Boer expansionism. Our own relations with the Boers were increasingly strained throughout this period. In particular the discovery of gold in the Transvaal in 1884 and the European powers' scramble for African colonies, which had started at the beginning of the decade, sharpened the hostility between Britain and the Afrikaners. When we finally subjugated the Boers in 1902, we were faced with controlling a large country with a partially hostile population. At the time it was seen as an enlightened act to follow our own example in Australia and Canada and give the country self-rule. It was seen equally as a gesture of great magnanimity and reconciliation between two peoples, prompted by a certain misguided sympathy for the 'plucky' Boer.

The result was the foundation in 1910 of the Union of South Africa, a self-governing dominion in which all the component parts, except the British-dominated Cape Colony, had whites-only franchises. From then on the history of South Africa was one of steady erosion of the non-white franchise until it disappeared altogether following the formal introduction of the apartheid concept in 1948.

In Rhodesia, the administration was undertaken by Cecil

Rhodes and the British South Africa Company in 1889 because the Government did not want to incur the cost of what seemed risky ventures into Mashonaland and Matabeleland. When the Company's Royal Charter expired in 1923 Rhodesia was formally annexed as a British colony. But no British colonial administration was put in to take over the running of the country. The Rhodesians were instead offered either entry into the Union of South Africa or what was called 'responsible' Government, with certain supervisory powers reserved to Britain—powers which, by the time of the 1961 Constitution, had for all practical purposes disappeared. When the Rhodesians chose the latter, power was by definition placed in the hands of a white minority who espoused racialist policies, though these fell far short of formal apartheid. In 1930, the Land Apportionment Act was passed with Britain's assent and Rhodesia divided into European and African areas. Many in Britain believed that this was a means of protecting the black population's land rather than the basis for racial discrimination which it subsequently became.

The development of the economy strengthened the position of the whites. Before the war, two-thirds of all European investment in Africa was going south of the Sahara and, in particular, to the mining areas of Southern and Central Africa. This trend continued after the Second World War. In the 1940s and 1950s the region experienced an economic boom stimulated by the influx of thousands of white settlers who were discouraged by conditions in post-war Western Europe. Those who went to Rhodesia reinforced the racial gulf which existed already. They boosted the white population of Rhodesia from about 50,000 in 1945 to some quarter of a million. It is often from this group that the strongest resistance has come to any move towards majority rule.

There were always contradictions and inconsistencies in British colonial policy towards Africa. This is hardly surprising given the differing interests and pressures which had to be accommodated. The central contradiction sprang from applying to Africa policies of self-government which derived from our experience in Canada and Australia, where the bulk of the population had been settlers from Europe. But in the African colonies the aspirations of the majority were not compatible with white settler self-government. In the Central African Federation, set up in 1953, Britain tried to create a multi-racial counterweight to South Africa, where the Afrikaner Nationalist Party had recently won power. This was an attempt to reconcile the irreconcilable. Inevitably the Federation dis-integrated because it proved impossible to accommodate within a single framework a racialist Southern Rhodesia and two territories where black aspirations were later to be realised in the independent nations of Zambia and Malawi.

It is this contradiction, and the ambiguity in British atti-tudes which it generated, that explains why, on the one hand, British policy enabled our relationship with Africa for the most part to evolve from one of colonialism to that of a mature partnership between equals within the framework of the Commonwealth; and, on the other, led us to abandon control, first in South Africa, and then in Rhodesia.

A similar ambiguity persists today in British policy towards Africa in the post-colonial era. There are sectors of British public opinion which seem oblivious to the feelings of the black majority and their wish for freedom and which identify ex-clusively with the white minority regimes in Southern Africa. This identification readily finds political expression in Britain and has not only influenced the commitment and policy of successive Governments but it has meant that our opposition as a nation to apartheid and our determination to bring about eventual majority rule has at times been seen to be at best equivocal. As a result Britain's generally good colonial record in Africa has become tarnished and our motives suspect. The challenge for a Labour Government which, as a matter of conviction and policy, is implacably opposed to racialism in all its forms is to point the way unswervingly to where the future of Africa must lie. This is not only a moral obligation: it is the assertion of our national interest. We must make it un-equivocally clear that we are now committed to doing every-thing possible to enable Africans to win their legitimate rights in Southern Africa.

While the pressure on South Africa mounts, the pressure on those countries which have economic links with South Africa to use those links to bring about change grows correspondingly. Britain, with its enormous economic stake in the Republic, is, in one sense, well placed to use those links judiciously and constructively to bring pressure on South Africa to moderate her policies. But, conversely, the very closeness of our economic relationship makes us dangerously vulnerable. Our huge economic involvement in a Republic whose future is uncertain and where the risk of social disruption is high is not only bad politics: it has now become economically risky too.

As regards investment, figures are not easily obtainable but it is generally understood that the total stock of UK investment including portfolio investment in South Africa measured in market-values is of the order of £5,000 million. This is probably double that of the United States or of Germany and greatly exceeds that of France or any other Western country.

As far as trade is concerned, our relationship is also closer than that of our partners. In 1976 British exports to South Africa were worth £653 million, somewhat lower than those of the United States and Germany; while our imports, at £612 million, were in round figures about double those of Japan, the United States and Germany. But another very important consideration is that our exports to black Africa (£1,329 million in 1976) and our imports from black Africa (£1,058 million in 1976) are now almost double the exports to and imports from South Africa.

At the moment we are in the position of depending on South Africa far more than is healthy if we are to pursue consistent and viable foreign and economic policies. But since we already have economic links with South Africa, we should use them positively to bring about change. British companies have a major role in ensuring good industrial relations in South Africa. The EEC Code of Conduct, with its emphasis on the development of collective bargaining in which black African workers would participate through independent trade unions of their choice, is an important step towards ensuring that British companies operating in South Africa understand the potentially positive role they could play in that society. A White Paper commending the Code formally to companies was published in May 1978. We are trying hard to persuade other OECD countries such as the US and Japan to adopt the Code. The existence of the Code is also an opportunity for British trade unions to play a part by urging British parent companies to adopt the practices it advocates.

In investment and in trade Britain faces a painful dilemma in its relationship with South Africa. We must reduce our over-dependence on that country economically. We stand to lose more than most if things go wrong. Prudent businessmen and prudent investors, no less than the British Government, should be taking a hard look at their South African connections.

A universal ban on trade with South Africa would cause major problems and higher unemployment in British exporting industries—notably in the high technology and machinery sectors—and would also disrupt industries at present dependent on imports of South African raw materials—principally chrome, manganese, platinum and other minerals. Our economic links with South Africa could not therefore disappear overnight without causing grave dislocation to the domestic economy and having severe repercussions on the level of employment. One complicating factor is the extent to which the economy of South Africa interfaces with the economies of the surrounding black African states. Lesotho and Swaziland are obvious examples but Botswana and Mozambique are particularly dependent. An independent Namibia and Zimbabwe would also be closely related and even Zambia and Malawi are indirectly affected. This linkage is one which would certainly raise immense difficulties in pursuing economic sanctions. It does, however, tend to make South Africa more aware of the need to work with black Africans and tends to demonstrate the absurdity as well as the indefensibility of apartheid.

We have to weigh up all these factors in evolving a consistent policy with a firm moral base. This is more easily said than done. It is a matter of finely tuned judgments relating principles to the means which must be deployed to put them into effect. Racialism in Southern Africa presents us with a sustained challenge which we shall not overcome in months or even a couple of years. The goal is the transition to a free and demo-cratic society based on equality before the law and human rights for all its people. We must not allow the very great difficulties which will inevitably confront us to diminish the force of our commitment.

In South Africa the promotion of human rights means the right of all people, regardless of colour, to live and work in peace, equality and mutual respect within the framework of a society founded on democratic majority rule. An integral part of this commitment is the conviction that societies of this kind can yet be created by peaceful means, although time is now desperately short in which to do it.

Violence is a last resort and one which is unlikely to be openly supported by the Western democracies. To advocate or legitimise violence runs counter to the whole system of values which we are pledged to sustain. But as long as a repressive system of white minority rule, impervious to peaceful political pressures, remains in existence, it will inevitably generate frustration and a sense of humiliation on such a scale that the black African populations will understandably be driven in increasing numbers to violence and the armed struggle. We cannot brand such Africans as the enemies of democracy and as disciples of Moscow merely because they are fighting for their rights. The defeat of Portuguese colonialism by freedom fighters supported by Soviet arms led inevitably to a marxist-orientated Government in Mozambique, although it is fiercely African-nationalist and non-aligned. The chaos in Angola and the subsequent civil war triggered the first Cuban involvement and Russian adventures in Africa, followed by the reassertion of Soviet power in the Horn of Africa through the use of Cuba as a surrogate. There are grave dangers in seeing the conflict in Africa as a straight fight between the forces of Soviet communism and those of Western democracy. In Zaire the basic issue is bad government, and political instability, in Shaba stemming from the Lunda tribe who cover Angolo, Zaire and Zambia. It plays straight into the hands of the Soviets to portray these conflicts in exclusively East-West terms. They will then be able convincingly to depict the West as morally bankrupt and supporters of apartheid. Our task, if we are to remain true to our democratic and human values, is to demonstrate beyond any shadow of a doubt that democratic change can be brought about rapidly and effectively by peaceful means. This involves using the authority of the United Nations and encouraging Africans to develop their own negotiated solutions.

In South Africa, our task is to establish how best we can encourage a peaceful evolution of society based on a serious programme of internal reforms. Hitherto, the instruments of moral and political persuasion which the international community has used have included public condemnation and progressive South African isolation at the United Nations. The discouragement of sporting contacts has had an undoubted influence on white South Africans. The mandatory arms embargo imposed in the aftermath of the tragic death of Steve Biko in 1977 served to heighten the tensions between South Africa and the international community. South African responses have so far been to tinker at the edges, but to stick adamantly to the fundamentals of apartheid. The minor changes so far introduced are totally inadequate to the scale of reforms needed. For Britain with its economic links the dilemma is particularly sensitive. One response is to try and ensure that where we do have British involvement we use that involvement in a positive way to break through apartheid. This is not a justification for new investment but at least a way of using existing investment. The EEC Code of Conduct offers a chance to attack racialism at the place of work, for instance by laying down conditions to ensure not only that black employees can freely form or join trade unions and take part in collective bargaining, but that they will also be paid a decent basic wage, receive the same rate for the job as white employees, have vastly improved access to training schemes, job advancement and fringe benefits, and in general enjoy equal working conditions with whites in, as far as possible, a desegregated environment.

The Code is but one of the pressures which it is vital to apply if a strategy for peaceful change is to be credible and successful. In the last analysis, we and the other Western democracies can only justify our economic stake in South Africa if it can be used, and be seen to be used, as an effective instrument for promoting change: abolition of the Immorality Act and the Pass Laws, the most deeply offensive overt signs of apartheid, and of detention and restrictions without trial are minimal early steps which must come quickly if any hope of peaceful change is to be kept alive. Without hope there is only desperation and desperation is the crucible of violence—urban and rural guerrilla violence.

The new thrust of President Carter's Administration's policy towards the African continent and in particular the United States's declared determination to see a democratic society evolve peacefully in South Africa is an additional and powerful factor for peaceful change. Previously, the United States had tended to adopt a policy of benign neglect. If their influence, authority and strength is now harnessed to a serious strategy of well-thought-out evolutionary change then there is still a chance that violence can be averted.

Change of this kind will not take place overnight. We are attempting to transform human behaviour, to alter prejudices and practices which have become ingrained in the last century and a half. If change does not come from within, the pressures to compel it from without will become irresistible, facing the international community with momentous and difficult decisions. In the United Nations the pressure for mandatory economic sanctions will inevitably grow.

Yet it is no good imposing sanctions only as a moral gesture or simply to punish recalcitrant behaviour. We must count the cost of our actions—to others as well as to ourselves—and adjust them to our goals. We obviously do not want to introduce measures the effect of which will be to drive white South Africans into acts of desperation where they would not only resist change in any form, but would produce a far more repressive regime even than exists already. There is nothing glamorous in violence. The liberation struggle in South Africa if it were to depend on violence would be bloodier than anywhere else in the world. The problem is that of locating and then treading a narrow path between driving the South Africans into a fortress within and around which millions would suffer for who knows how long, and bringing the whites to realise that it is in their own best interests to adopt internal policies which are acceptable to the majority and so to the international community.

Under the UN Charter, the Security Council is empowered

to require action by all member states if the Council makes a determination of the existence of a threat to the peace, breach of the peace or act of aggression. On only four occasions in the history of the United Nations has the Council invoked Chapter 7. The first was in the Middle East in 1948; the second was in Korea in 1950; and the third was in Rhodesia in 1966.

In 1977 the UN for the fourth time invoked Chapter 7 over South Africa. The decision to go for a Chapter 7 determination was a very serious one to take. It was a measure of the profound concern at what had been happening in South Africa over the years. The basis of the determination is the view that South Africa's acquisition of weapons in the current situation constitutes a threat to international peace and security. The resolution places a binding obligation on all United Nations member states to cease the supply of arms and military material to South Africa.

Ever since the Labour Government decision in 1964 Britain has operated a voluntary embargo on the export of arms to South Africa. When the Labour Government returned to power in 1974, one of the first things it did was to tighten up the implementation of that embargo, and to cancel the export licence for an outstanding Wasp helicopter. But while the British record has been good, some countries continued to supply arms. A mandatory embargo was long overdue. In its absence South Africa acquired a substantial range of modern military equipment and aircraft and developed a significant armament industry.

There are many voices now raised in favour of mandatory economic sanctions. Any economic sanctions will require careful thought and balanced judgment. Oil sanctions, for example, have implications for other parts of the world. It is not just the drafting of resolutions, but the consequences of resolutions which need to be worked carefully through. Southern Africa is a complex area, where economic interrelationships between countries have very important ramifications. Britain is already reviewing the area of its economic relations with South Africa with its European Community partners. We will honour our obligations to the UN and to our commitment to overcome apartheid. We will not be laggards, but on one issue we will, however, be resolute. Britain will not take measures unless they are supported not just by resolutions but in practice and if necessary in law by the main Western industrialised powers. We will carry our fair share of any burden in the international cause of bringing about peacefully a change in apartheid policies of South Africa. We could not, however, defend to our people taking economic action unilaterally, which could hurt employment prospects and our financial strength, only then to see other countries flouting the UN resolutions and filling the economic gap left by our decision.

We did this over Rhodesia for many years and at a heavy price, because we had a legal responsibility to lead the world. But despite the fact that Rhodesian sanctions were meant to have been applied under Chapter 7, many other countries did not fully apply them. The United States for a number of years specifically excluded chrome imports from Rhodesia.

Over South Africa, we have moral responsibilities, but so too does the whole world. No one should be under any illusions as to the nature of the challenge facing the United Nations over South Africa. It is a challenge that will be with us not just for months but for years, and it will need courage, persistence and commitment; but if we hold firm then we can make a contribution to the peace of the world. For one thing is clear: if the course that is being followed in South Africa at the moment were to continue unchanged, then the consequences can only be a bitter division between the races and a bitter—and bloody—conflict between them.

7

The United Nations

The constant struggle to close the gap between aspiration and performance in the United Nations was described in 1955 by the then Secretary General Dag Hammarskjöld as making the difference between civilisation and chaos. Today, this gap between aspiration and performance remains and the danger of chaos is ever-present.

The United Nations has from its inception championed all the most fundamental human rights: the right to live without hunger or disease; in peace, free from conflict and the fear of nuclear, or any other kind of war.

Appalling and well-documented events naturally focus great attention worldwide on the abuse or absence of political, civil and legal rights: and on violations and degradations of the integrity of the person, though the sense of outrage over Chile and Uganda, to take but two examples, has not yet been matched by effective international action. But the global challenge of chronic poverty, malnutrition and disease ensures that we cannot escape our responsibility for economic and social rights.

Between 1952 and 1972 the gross product of the advanced industrialised nations increased by $1·82 trillion. The aggregate product of the underdeveloped world in 1972 was less than a third of this increase. This statistic is shocking enough, the reality behind even more so. It is generally agreed that more than 400 million people have an insufficient protein supply. About 70 million of them are immediately threatened by starvation. In some of the very poorest countries there is a 50 per cent infant mortality rate and the development of people's brains is literally stunted by protein and calorie insufficiencies. Most of the world's poor only have access to unsafe water. They are therefore chronically vulnerable to schistosomiasis, one of the symptoms of which is dysentery, and to filariasis, a leading cause of blindness and elephantiasis. In some areas of conflict the disruption of basic social and medical services poses a challenge to world health. We risk a recrudescence of smallpox in the Horn of Africa and a revival of the tsetse fly, which causes sleeping sickness, in East and Southern Africa. The human needs of the developing world are an inescapable challenge to us all and a central element in any foreign policy based on human rights.

To establish a fairer and more rational international economic order, both developed and developing nations must work together as equal partners. The dialogue, if it is to be successful, must be seen as a long-term sequence of negotiation on specific issues. The Governments of the industrialised democracies are at present under tremendous domestic political pressure to reduce rapidly high rates of unemployment. We need a greater frankness and realism in the dialogue; the present world recession has hit both developed and developing nations. The developing nations will easily become cynical and despairing if the developed world's actions run counter to its rhetoric. Those of us who represent the industrialised democracies are not entitled to use our economic difficulties as an excuse for abdicating from the dialogue. We must all try and ensure that we develop a long-term strategy which is credible and corrects the effects of some of the short-term decisions which we may feel compelled to take. If we continue into the future the present allocation of resources we will only perpetuate the existing imbalance between the developed and the developing world.

The United Nations rightly devotes a high priority (nearly 40 per cent of its net regular budget) to economic and social activities. Britain in addition to its own European Community aid programmes contributed in 1976 some $85 million to the UN's work in the economic and social field.

Despite the immense problems which still face us, in the crucial areas of poverty, hunger and disease, the United Nations has shown itself to be an effective and practical instrument. The institutions of the UN have also made a major technical contribution towards a more orderly international environment in, for instance, the fields of labour relations, posts and telecommunications, shipping, and civil aviation.

But in reducing conflict in the world, achieving peace and in restraining the armaments race the United Nations cannot claim that its performance has anywhere near matched its aspirations. It is worth examining the distribution of the total financial effort of the United Nations. The UN in New York, together with the all-important autonomous agencies, spent in 1976 some $2,200 million. Of the total UN financial commitment, only 8 per cent went on what can be summarised briefly as political, diplomatic and peace-keeping activities. If words uttered and words written were anything to go by, these activities would occupy a far higher position in our order of priorities than any others. We write and speak much about this area and yet spend relatively little on it, while the consequences of conflict are grievous for millions.

It is a regrettable fact of life that in institutional terms, the maintenance of world security is the most neglected activity within the United Nations. Health, hunger and poverty are issues on which member nations are prepared to concede an institutional competence and role for the UN. But with few exceptions security is seen as the preserve of national Governments. We are prepared to see our doctors, agriculturists, sociologists and economists working together and pooling their expertise within a UN institutional framework. But we are reluctant to see our Generals and our Admirals and our strategic thinkers working within such a framework on behalf of world security.

We are all familiar with our own national security problems. But there is all too little understanding of each other's security problems, fears, and objectives. As an international body, the UN ought to be able to foresee areas of dispute and act in time to prevent open conflict from breaking out. It should be able to act speedily to damp down a dispute in its early stages. The UN, if it is involved in a conflict, is usually involved late and with reluctance.

The United Nations is the only forum in which the whole

international community is represented. It has the right and the duty to be involved in disputes which threaten peace and stability whether on a regional or on a global scale. But to date it has lacked the necessary authority and commitment, which can only be given to it by its member states.

The member states of the UN are reluctant to make even modest commitments to international security arrangements. The resources devoted to peace-keeping are only a fraction of those employed in the UN organisation as a whole and the UN's role in peace-keeping has not been sufficiently recognised by the member states who have not been prepared to commit forces for UN service. These facts highlight the low priority we give to this area of the UN's activity.

The UN's overall record in the field of world security is one which we should be prepared to analyse critically, particularly now that the Cold War era of confrontation diplomacy is over and when the superpowers themselves now exchange detailed information on the most sensitive security issue of all, namely strategic nuclear weapons. What is needed is for the United Nations to stimulate a specialised and constructive dialogue between Governments on every aspect of world security in a way which would improve the ability of the international community to respond quickly and effectively in situations where action by the United Nations is required. If such a dialogue was in operation today, we could have been far better able to examine some of the detailed security problems which now confront us all in Africa.

The present limitations as well as the value of the UN in its peace-keeping role are clearly demonstrated by the situation in the Middle East and Cyprus, where the UN has made a massive, sustained, but all too frequently unappreciated effort over the years to keep the peace.

In the Middle East, the world still faces the most serious of all potential conflicts. The resurgence of fighting in South Lebanon in March 1978 was a sad reminder both of the urgency of finding a solution to the Middle East conflict as a whole and of the difficulties which the Lebanese Government faces in restoring peace and security in that country. Here was an opportunity, before the fighting developed, for the UN to anticipate conflict by arguing in the Security Council that the situation was a threat to peace. Nevertheless the eventual response of the United Nations showed flexibility and a potentially more effective attitude. The Security Council decision to send a force was taken over the weekend in a rapid and decisive manner, and without that action an escalation of the conflict looked inevitable. The United Nations has been involved diplomatically in the Middle East since 1947. Its involvement in security arrangements through UNEF and UNDOF have cost more than $269 million. In 1977 it cost around $98 million. The United Nations presence in the Middle East has been at times controversial, but without it there would have been even greater bloodshed and incidents.

In the debate since the 1967 Arab-Israeli war about the occupied territory, security issues have become of central importance and of deep and genuine concern. Hitherto nations have tended to equate security solely with the possession of territories. This is no longer the only relevant factor. Sophisticated electronic devices can now give a military security which nations had hitherto believed could only come from the physical occupation of territory. The monitoring techniques already in place in Sinai have made possible a measure of disengagement and lessened mistrust between Israel and Egypt. Confidence-building measures in the shape of demilitarised zones, zones of limited forces, surveillance and early warning systems, microwave links, could all be an essential component in any final settlement. The United Nations has a role to play, either by supervising and operating these devices, or even more importantly in promoting an informed public debate on the underlying technical security issues.

The danger of a United Nations peace-keeping involvement, initially to hold the ring, is that it can become an excuse for political inactivity or a substitute for serious negotiation. In Cyprus, as in the Middle East, the United Nations peace-keeping forces have reduced hostilities and provided time in which serious negotiations could and should have taken place. The present UN commitment in Cyprus cannot be taken for granted. In the last thirteen years of UNFICYP's existence, it has cost member states, by way of voluntary contributions, some

$200 million. Furthermore, the force is now seriously in deficit to the tune of some $50 million. The United Kingdom has contributed $45 million in men and in logistical support. In 1977 our contingent numbered 800 men and was the largest single contribution. The United Nations does not enjoy infinite resources, as the Secretary General's recent appeal for further contributions to this force makes plain, and the reserves will be further strained by the financial cost of peace-keeping in Southern Lebanon.

The United Nations cannot, therefore, either in Cyprus or in the Middle East, be used indefinitely as a cover for a stalemate in negotiations. It cannot continue to be seen as a last resort—a permanent crutch for maintaining a state of 'no peace, no war'. What the UN can do is to establish the political framework within which negotiations between the parties can take place and, through harnessing the initiatives of its member states and acting as a catalyst for their ideas, help to provide the impetus needed to break out of the present stalemate.

In Southern Africa, it has become increasingly clear that negotiated settlements which are internationally accepted and have the full support of the United Nations have the best chance of ending the violence and of achieving stable majority rule government. This is the hope for a future Zimbabwe and Namibia.

It is a truism that the UN is only what its members make of it. The paradox of the United Nations's role is that on the one hand it is indispensable in the search for peace and, on the other, limited in what it can achieve on its own initiative.

All British Governments, since 1945, have been pledged to support the ideals of the United Nations Charter, which are largely the traditional ideals of Western democracies. To promote the greatest possible international support for those ideals is clearly not only in our own national interest, but also in the interests of the free world.

In supporting the UN as it stands, despite its imperfections, we are maintaining the best sort of world organisation we are likely to get. The charter was drafted at a time when Western influence and British prestige were at their zenith. Were it to be rebuilt now from scratch, the structure of the organisation would be very different. It would not be so favourable to Britain or to many of our nearest allies. Britain would be unlikely to be one of the five permanent members of the Security Council.

The founding fathers gave, through the veto power of the permanent member, a safeguard against the irresponsible use of the United Nations. For all the frustrations associated with the power of the veto, at times when it has stopped the United Nations from going forward in what appeared to be sensible directions, it has also stopped the United Nations from following the decline of the League of Nations. It has given the UN a strength and a basic stability, and made certain that, particularly in a world of vast inequalities of power between member states, the influence of the superpowers was felt throughout the organisation. An organisation that was purely representative of the majority, which did not take account of the weight of the superpower and the realities of power in the world, would not have been able to play as important a role as it has.

The balance of influence within the United Nations organisation has shifted radically in the past fifteen years. As a result, the developing countries have acquired a dominant role in most areas of the organisation's work. Britain and like-minded states are now very much in the minority. In 1970, we saw the start of the United Nations development decade. In the years since then, African affairs and the North-South dialogue have dominated regular assemblies and two special sessions. East and West Germany have joined the organisation and the People's Republic of China has finally taken the place of Nationalist China. The United Nations is now in the third stage of its history.

In its early years, it became primarily a forum in which the Cold War could be fought out with the West enjoying a comfortable majority. At the beginning of the 1960s, the emphasis changed: the thawing of the Cold War and the granting of independence to the majority of former colonies shifted the UN's attention to colonial questions for the next decade. During the most recent period, the Third World majority have used their position in the General Assembly to focus, quite rightly, on development and the call for a new international economic order. North-South issues will remain a central subject of UN discussion for the foreseeable future.

Much of the UN's work on economic and social questions goes unsung or is taken for granted. Parts of the United Nations system are essential to the modern world's operation and present few problems. We rarely celebrate the work of the World Health Organisation, yet it has virtually achieved the public health dream, the total eradication of smallpox. Massive changes have taken place as a result of the World Health Organisation activity over eradicating malaria, although there are many other illnesses still to be conquered that are a major problem for the world as a whole. The World Health Organisation is only one of the specialised organisations which has had a successful record. In looking at United Nations activity we should look at the whole picture instead of concentrating only on the political activity in New York.

We shall continue to support the invaluable work of these specialised agencies and the economic and social work of the UN itself, but public opinion is readier to judge the organisation by its failures, which are remorselessly publicised, than by its successes, which are very seldom noticed. Many attempt to write off the United Nations merely because of its failure to live up to some of the more ambitious expectations of its founders or to the over-idealistic standards they have themselves set for it. It is far more profitable to accept the United Nations for what it is and recognise that, however imperfect, it fulfils an essential need as the only forum designed to consider world issues. Our main task is to ensure that it performs this role as effectively as possible and to strengthen it where we can. Its friends must be prepared to criticise it and not leave criticism just to its enemies. It is often the limitations imposed on it by its members which have prevented full realisation of the original aims of the Charter. The Charter needs to be upheld and championed—it represents the single most significant step which has been taken in the direction of world peace and for this reason alone requires our support.

Britain has an interest in seeing a strong and effective UN, as an agency for preventing or moderating international conflict, as a forum for discussion of major world issues, an instrument for development and for establishing world services in a wide variety of fields and as a means of promoting British influence and views on many of these issues. For all these purposes, we wish to see a stronger world organisation with a better peace-keeping capacity than at present; better equipped for serious negotiation on issues in dispute; better organised to undertake its many functional tasks; and better adapted especially to resolve the many North-South issues which increasingly dominate world politics.

The preservation of our national security will be affected only indirectly by what we do at the United Nations, but many other aims of our foreign policy—the resolution of disputes, an ordered North-South dialogue, disarmament, arms control, promotion of human rights, the advancement and regularisation of the rule of law, the organisation of world services—all these are most effectively pursued within the universal framework of the UN. All these contribute to our own security and economic benefit, as well as to the development of a more harmonious international community.

On economic questions, we have an interest in using the negotiating framework the UN provides. Third World countries have made it clear that it is their preferred forum for the continuation of the North-South dialogue. We should therefore be willing to treat the Assembly at least as a steering committee for the dialogue, which can regularly review the situation, even though we may sometimes wish that negotiations on specific issues should take place in a more specialised forum, usually within the UN system. One of the areas that we are discussing at the moment is how we can get an international dialogue about energy problems.

No one would deny that the UN has been less effective in maintaining the world's peace over the last thirty years than most people hoped when it was founded. Some of the reasons are obvious: differences among the superpowers, the unwillingness of members to obey United Nations calls when vital national security interests are at stake. In many cases the threat to the peace or even major conflicts have not been brought to the notice of the world body. The conflicts in Vietnam, Nigeria,

Angola, and most recently the dispute between Somalia and Ethiopia were all suitable for UN action, but were never brought to the Security Council. Over the Horn of Africa the OAU was given the task of mediation; African states preferred to use their regional body rather than the UN. This might have worked if the dispute had not involved Russia and Cuba, but once they were involved it seemed obvious that a regional body like the OAU did not have the same resources and influence as the UN. A major condition for more effective UN action is that the organisation should become involved at a far earlier stage. One need, if this is to be achieved, is for member states other than those directly involved to be willing to bring situations to the Security Council when appropriate. This is clearly envisaged in the Charter under Article 35, but is in practice very rarely done. All nations should be readier to do so where necessary.

There is too a need for the Secretariat to keep all crisis situations all over the world under continuous review, so that the Secretary General himself may bring matters to the Security Council, where appropriate under Article 99. There is a need for regular discussion amongst Governments, within the Council and outside, on such crisis situations before they reach the point of full-scale war. We should consider means to achieve this, including the interesting proposal by the Canadians for regular Council meetings at foreign minister level.

If we could promote discussion before disputes have taken place sometimes in private session, it could lead to proposals for a more active UN involvement before fighting has broken out. This might take the form of calls for further negotiations between the parties or for the appointment of a mediator or the despatch of a special representative of the Secretary General to promote a settlement.

We need to define guidelines on peace-keeping for UN forces in the Committee of 33; and encourage member states, if they are inclined, to organise and train parts of their armed forces on a compatible basis so as to be able to take part in peace-keeping operations at short notice when called on to do so. There are already some countries which do that. And above all, we in Britain should be prepared to propose and support the establishment of the new UN forces in suitable cases. In addition to our Cyprus contribution we supplied logistic support from Cyprus for the UN forces in the Lebanon because we felt it was important to respond to the request from the Secretary General.

Another important UN activity is the International Commission which was set up in 1949 for the development and codification of international law. The Commission has been responsible for, among other things, the international conventions on diplomatic relations, consular relations, the law of treaties, and it is handling at present the question of the succession of states to international treaties.

The Human Rights Convention and the two International Covenants have been formulated in the Third Committee. The disarmament treaties have been negotiated in the Conference of the Committee on Disarmament. Some of the work of the Sixth Committee, such as the work on Principles of Friendly Relations, the Definition of Aggression, although not strictly speaking a matter of law-making, can be regarded as attempts to establish an international code of conduct.

These are vital. They provide the essential basis to the nuts and bolts of UN activity and the structural framework for international stability and international peace. If we did not have this unglamorous activity going on underneath the surface all the time, we would soon notice its absence.

One of our major aims as a country and as a Government is to see a strengthening of the United Nations capacity in the protection of human rights. For many years, United Nations activity in this field took the form of drafting declarations, conventions and covenants which, though usually passed by large majorities, normally had no perceptible impact on the protection of human rights in any part of the world. There was therefore an increasing discussion of means of improving their implementation. The convention on the elimination of all forms of racial discrimination, which came into force in 1969, first created machinery to ensure implementation of undertakings made. The two covenants, one of which came into force in 1976, established similar machinery which is now in action. It is important to ensure that such machinery operates effectively. United Nations selectivity, criticised in some quarters, has been very evident in this field. The international criticism of Israel, South Africa and Chile has been rightly pronounced in every United Nations forum, yet there has been a marked reluctance to arraign other offenders such as the Eastern European countries or even some developing countries.

Some countries whose human rights record is under challenge counter-attack with the criticism that the West is over-concerned with civil and political rights, at the expense of the economic and social rights which can represent the difference between life and death for many of their own people. It is true that we must be careful of just trying to inject liberal values from relatively affluent societies into poor countries. There is a hollow ring in some countries about our championing of human rights if it is not accompanied by concern for their economic and developmental plight. Economic rights, social rights and human rights are indivisible—and we should not try to separate them or try to justify poorer countries' neglect of human rights. To do so would be to reduce the moral case for ensuring that the richer countries of the world redistribute resources to the poorer countries of the world. It is necessary to end selectivity over human rights, to champion human rights in all parts of the world. We must attack right-wing abuses as in Chile, but also attack human rights abuses in communist countries. We must be prepared to arraign ourselves on the side of the black majorities who find themselves racially discriminated against in Southern Africa, but we must not flinch either from not only criticising racialism in our own country, but also ensuring that other black countries criticise the grotesque excesses of countries such as Uganda.

Developing countries will continue to make the demand for economic and social rights a defence for their position on civil and political rights, but abuses of civil and political rights can always, if the will exists, be prevented by relatively simple political decisions.

Economic and social rights require adequate economic resources and they require positive action in the transfer of such resources. The Western countries will need to emphasise the importance they attach to both types of rights.

The United Kingdom will strive to ensure that the bettering of human rights is a central concern of the United Nations. We will seek to improve the existing procedures and machinery while recognising that a more fundamental requirement is a change of attitudes. We have outlined in Resolution 1503 a confidential process whereby the UN Commission on Human Rights and its Sub-Commission consider communications to the Secretary General from individuals or groups of people which appear to reveal a consistent pattern of gross and reliably attested violations of human rights. We will do all we can to make this procedure operate more effectively, which means we will consider other mechanisms to bring about better implementation. We will support proposals for improving the workings of the Human Rights Commission, including the suggestion that it should meet more frequently. We will continue to support the proposal for a High Commissioner for Rights. We will send our permanent representative at the UN, or a Minister if appropriate, to represent us at appropriate important meetings of the Commission. We will promote discussion of the most frequent types of abuse of human rights.

Above all, we will stick to our policies, and when we take a stand against a country that has abused human rights and sometimes take economic measures, we must not expect results to appear overnight. We must be prepared to hold a policy for three, four or five years and sometimes at some economic price. Chile is a prime example of the need to hold firm to a steady course.

The role of the United Nations as a central institution for the discussion of worldwide issues is likely to increase rather than to decline as time goes on. Many global issues in addition to peace and war have got to be confronted. Nuclear proliferation, disaster relief, the sea bed, the world environment, energy, disarmament, development, monetary questions, world resources, the list is endless. In some cases there are specialised institutions, usually UN agencies, confronting these issues. For others discussions can only take place in the United Nations itself.

Britain already plays an active and a positive role in such debates. We must be willing to see institutional reforms to make the United Nations better equipped to deal with such topics. We must continue to take an active part in restructuring the economic and social sectors of the United Nations system; to improve its efficiency. But above all, we must retain our commitment to the United Nations as an institution.

8

World Poverty

Utopian pledges and unrealistic dreams bedevil discussion of aid and development policy. There is confusion between what is ultimately desirable, and what is practicable within a realistic timescale; there is confusion between what it is in our interests to do, and what we should give as world citizens to others. There is a belief that there are simple divisions between a rich 'North' and a poor 'South', that there exists a 'Third World', and that every country is in one camp or in another. In fact there are no such easy categories. A rich developing country can have great poverty and extremes of wealth within it; a poor country can spread the available resources fairly to all its citizens.

While most of what the Government advocates in establishing a new economic order is very much to this country's advantage, self-interest will never provide a sufficient justification for that redistribution which is a long-term necessity. There is a moral dimension that we should not be afraid to identify and draw upon. A country that develops an attitude and an ethos which ignores poverty and inequality in the world soon ignores poverty and inequality on its own doorstep. It is a comfortable and seductive theory that you can concentrate on your problems at home first and only then look outwards to the world, but it is a delusion. If one once constricts the national horizon it will not be easy later to widen it out.

A situation in which the rich nations maintain a monopoly of technological and industrial skills will never be acceptable to the rest of the world. An American socialist, Michael Harrington, wrote recently that the United States is what Paul Samuelson called a 'cathedral economy' in relation to the Third World: 'They [the Third World countries] will increasingly specialise in the laborious tasks of transforming raw materials into commodities; we will think, control, manage.'* According to Harrington, the division of labour in the world is becoming polarised. Dirty and unpleasant manufacturing tasks (such as the refining of raw materials) are now being carried out in the developing countries, while the developed countries are concerned less and less with actual manufacturing and more and more with high technology and research, management and the provision of services.

On the surface, and seen from the comfortable vantage point of a Western middle-class lifestyle, this looks rational. *They*, the Third World, have plentiful cheap labour; *we*, the industrial West, have skills and technology. Together, so the theory goes, we can develop the world in a perfect partnership. Yet that 'partnership' can easily become a euphemism for retaining and even buttressing massive inequality. We must remember that the developing countries have their own clear views on how they wish that partnership to develop. We must be prepared to listen to what they are saying and to take account of their views. We need to move forward together, recognising that the present position will only be improved by peaceful and rational co-operation.

The inequalities which exist today are the direct result of the uneven pattern of world industrial development and population growth which has emerged over the last two hundred years. Historically, the present levels of inequality between nations are unprecedented. Around 1850 the average per capita income of the countries now regarded as developed or advanced was some $150, while the rest of the world had income per capita in the region of $100. In contrast, Professor Jan Tinbergen, the Nobel Prizewinning economist, estimates the ratio between average incomes in countries accounting for the richest and poorest 10 per cent of the earth's population at 13:1.† The inequalities are simply the most obvious feature of a process of development which has become increasingly global, both in the

* *The Vast Majority: A Journey to the World's Poor* by Michael Harrington (Simon and Schuster, New York, 1977).

† *Reshaping the International Order: A Report to the Club of Rome*, co-ordinated by Jan Tinbergen (E. P. Dutton, New York, 1976).

sense of now involving virtually all corners of the earth and in the sense of ever-greater interdependence. Given the development of modern communications, one can now literally get an overall view of the world economy as if from a satellite and through statistics trace out many of its economic interconnections. One can also see how national boundaries are of less and less significance as the process and integration of production become more and more international. Domestic and international issues thus get merged. We in Britain are increasingly challenged to see how our own role in this world economy is changing, as we struggle to keep control over our own part of it, when so many of the crucial worldwide influences — technological advance, international relocations of production, capital flows — are largely outside the control of any one or even all Governments.

This raises a number of challenges. How should we adapt international institutions and economic relationships to the realities of the world economy as they are emerging? How should we develop political and economic forms of management to ensure efficient and democratic control over this enormous and complex process of interactions and development? How should we in Britain ensure that our own say in this management protects our interests? How can we ensure for the Third World a reasonable voice in this management and sufficient control over the process that the worst inequalities created or persisting are eradicated within the foreseeable future? These are questions to which we ought to be addressing ourselves.

The distinction between developed and developing countries is likely to become blurred in the next few years. We must never forget that action taken by the better-off developing countries against the developed countries can have disastrous effects on the least developed countries; and that those better-off developing countries have an important part to play in setting up a better and more rational world economy. Beyond the moral dimension, we must be hard-headed about what *we* want, yet sympathetic to the aspirations of the developing countries.

We need first a careful analysis of what the 'Third World' is, and we need specific rather than general policies to match its diversities. There is no simple standard definition of *developing countries.* The Development Assistance Committee of the OECD, an important international group, has described the developing countries as:

All countries in Africa except South Africa, in America except the United States and Canada, in Asia except Japan and China, in Oceania except Australia and New Zealand. In Europe the list comprises Cyprus, Gibraltar, Greece, Portugal, Spain, Turkey and Yugoslavia.

But we should guard against lumping all developing countries together in one basket. Twenty-five developing countries were identified as having particularly severe long-term restraints on development according to three basic criteria—per capita gross domestic product of $100 or less, a share of manufacturing of 10 per cent or less of GDP, and 20 per cent or fewer literate persons aged fifteen or over. The twenty-five were internationally recognised at UNCTAD II (1968) and in the UN General Assembly in 1971 as *least* developed countries or LLDCs. They were: Afghanistan, Benin, Bhutan, Botswana, Burma, Chad, Ethiopia, Guinea, Haiti, Laos, Lesotho, Malawi, the Republic of Maldives, Mali, Nepal, Niger, Rwanda, Sikkim, Somalia, Sudan, Tanzania, Uganda, Upper Volta, Western Samoa and the Yemen Arab Republic. In 1975 Bangladesh, the Central African Empire, The Gambia and the People's Democratic Republic of the Yemen were added. The LLDCs are the poorest of the poor and in their case there can be no doubt of the overriding moral case in favour of our aiding them.

Another common term in this field is the 'Group of 77'—or G77 for short—which is the name given to the developing countries acting together as a group to put forward their policies, particularly at meetings of UNCTAD and other UN forums. The number of '77' is ever-increasing; in November 1977 it stood at 115.

Some 'less developed countries' (LDCs) such as the OPEC countries and the so-called 'super-competitives' are in many respects doing well. Take Saudi Arabia. If, for the sake of argument, we assume a doubling of oil prices, a doubling of the quantity of oil produced, a population growth of 3 per cent per annum, and 3 per cent per annum per capita growth in the non-oil sector, then Saudi income per head in 1990 would be just over $12,000 at 1976 prices. This compares with a projected $11,250 per capita income for the United States. Total GNP would have quadrupled in Saudi Arabia by 1990; GNP per head would have increased by 2·7 times. Saudi Arabia is perhaps an exceptional case, but other countries such as Mexico, Brazil and South Korea are growing rich very fast. Towards the end of the century some of them will compare very favourably with developed countries now. At the other end of the scale, the LLDCs remain desperately poor; and then there are countries such as India which has two separate economies, a rapidly growing industrial sector co-existing with acute rural poverty—the world's problem epitomised in one country.

What is happening now is that, in a situation of basic economic inequality in the world, the Group of 77 are demanding structural change. To them the developed countries appear not to be listening. Yet to us, while some of their demands are fair and reasonable, others are clearly unreasonable. Yet without a negotiated change in some basic areas of the world economy— something which is both desirable and attainable—we shall face anarchy and chaos by the end of the century.

It is pessimistic to assume that we will go on as we are going now until the year 2000 but, while instinctively distrusting extrapolations, we should try to develop just such a hypothetical scenario. The first twist of the spiral could already have begun, with the present long-drawn-out world recession. In the developed countries we see that there is increasing pressure for protectionism, already the refuge of many underdeveloped countries. The next move could—in this pessimistic scenario— be the rich world failing to increase, or instead actually decreasing, the flow of aid to the developing countries. Thus protectionist measures in the developed world would hit at the exports of the developing countries and their growth would be further hit by a cut-back in aid for investment in modernising old industries and establishing new ones.

The markets in developing countries for the exports of the

developed world would cease to grow. This would add to the recession in the developed countries and, much more importantly, would bring developing countries to a situation in which they would have great difficulty in repaying their debts. The indebtedness of some countries is already a cause for concern. Some would be forced to default and this action would have grave consequences for the world banking system. The net effect could be severe deflation on a world scale. Living standards could plummet everywhere. In the developing countries political extremists and demagogues would vie with each other in making impossible promises about better things to come. Governments would change repeatedly, administration would deteriorate, extremism would mount and the major threat to the world would be chaos rather than conflict. The rich would be less rich and the poor would become even more desperately poor.

In the developed countries unemployment, already a major problem, would act as a catalyst for increased racism and xenophobia and feelings of extreme nationalism and intolerance would manifest themselves in total disregard for the developing world. As a consequence of chaos or as a diversion from it conflict would break out, fuelled by the trade in arms.

The picture is one which many people would not consider to be totally implausible. Too many of the current trends in the world economy point in this direction. We ignore the threat and pooh-pooh the extrapolation at our peril.

The actual outcome of these trends will, one suspects, be different, having deliberately stressed all the most pessimistic aspects of the present situation. But the trends are there. Take arms, for example. The developing countries, particularly in the Middle East and Africa, are spending more and more on arms. The developing countries' share of world military expenditure rose from 6 per cent in 1966 to 15 per cent in 1976. We in the developed world encourage this trend – we talk about restraining our own arms sales but we have as yet evolved no coherent plan, no agreement among ourselves, and so we compete against each other and justify industrial sales on the basis that if we did not sell other countries would.

According to the 1977 SIPRI publication *World Armaments:*

The Nuclear Threat, the countries of the Third World spent a total of $51,000 million on defence in 1976:

Middle East	$27,300 million
Far East	$6,420 million
South America	$5,600 million
South Asia	$4,000 million
Africa	$6,490 million
Central America	$1,190 million

This is almost three times as much as the amount which they received in development aid, despite the continued efforts of donors to increase the aid flow. It is a trend which should be reversed if we are to speed up world economic and social progress. It is manifestly absurd that increased development assistance from the industrialised countries should indirectly help military activities in the Third World.

If any of these projections provide an even remotely plausible scenario of the economic state of the world in 1990, then the necessity to plan to avoid them needs no stressing. The obvious alternative is for the countries of the world to sit down together and agree on a new and rational basis for organising the world's economy and managing its resources.

The first prerequisite of any policy directed at improving and rationalising the world's economic system is that the world should be taken out of its current recession. If the world economy as a whole were growing, the effect on the developing world, both directly and through the impact on the industrialised countries, would be dramatic, and much more significant than any conceivable increase in aid. In a sense the best thing we in this country could do to help the developing world would be to restore full employment here and get our own economy moving again. This would immediately increase markets for developing countries' goods, make it easier for balance of payments deficits to be reduced, and improve the world financial climate generally, so that resource transfers to the developing world would be easier and there would be fewer pressures for protectionism. But we cannot, acting on our own, restore the world economy; this too is something which depends on concerted international action. There is no greater challenge to the world's politicians than this issue at present. The restraint of OPEC countries in the face of demands from some of their members for an increase in oil prices is a good example of an act by one group of countries which is in the broader interest of the world economy rather than in their own short-term interest.

Since the shock of the 1973 five-fold increase in oil prices, and the Middle East war, there has in fact been a less confrontational attitude among the nations of the world on many issues affecting trade and aid policy. It is important that this spirit of negotiation should be fostered and developed. We must all recognise the effect our policies can have on the rest of the world. The developed countries have OECD to research and refine their policies. There is a strong case for similar expertise to be developed to serve the interests of the Group of 77. On both sides there is a need for better research on the background to policies, and more comprehensive study of the consequences of what is proposed. A better-informed dialogue is in everyone's interest if we are to concentrate on achievable reforms and not take up unyielding positions on either side.

A dramatic change that has taken place in the world economy in the last few years has been the shift of a number of productive processes to the developing countries, so that today's major challenge to the developed countries is how they cope with 'adjustment'. For Britain one of the central issues confronting us is to adjust our long-established—and now not necessarily competitive—industrial base to competition from newly established and sometimes super-competitive industries of the developing world. There will be industries which we have to prop up in the short term, but which in the long term will have to contract in the face of competition from low labour cost countries.

It is vital that Government, trade unions and employers in this country should face up to future international realities. The right strategy will differ between one industry and another but diversification, new investment and retraining are all important if we are to anticipate future international trends. It is something which we should do as an act of self-interest, yet it is in many ways the most difficult problem we face. It raises in acute form questions of economics—the best way for resources to be allocated nationally and internationally; questions of politics—the way we respond to new demands of developing countries whose very success is often based on aid and technology we have provided; and of how we organise our society—the jobs we do, the economic prospects we can offer our children and the way we plan for, explain and manage inevitable transition.

The vision of 'floods of imports' from developing countries exploiting a pool of cheap labour is evocative; but it does not tell the whole story. Productivity is at the heart of the matter and underlines our failure to compete in many sectors: the evidence is that those developed countries which have been most successful in increasing productivity in particular industries have also fared best in maintaining employment or minimising the loss of employment. The plain fact is that with the comparative advantage in abundant and increasingly educated labour which many developing countries enjoy, joined to the advantages they have as 'late arrivers' of being able to cut technological corners, the developing countries will inevitably pose mounting competition to the simpler forms of manufacturing in OECD countries. One of the paradoxes is that frequently our industries in these sectors—not only in this country but elsewhere in the EEC and in the US—use immigrant labour to compete with the products of the immigrants' countries of origin. As a result of these trends many of our basic industries will not be able to continue into the 1990s without radical change and their share of the market is bound to decline. The manufacturing labour force is likely to continue to fall. We prop up some industries on social and employment grounds, and understandably so, but short-term help must be countered by new investment and the creation of new jobs. In the long run the cost of subsidising industries which can no longer hold their own in fair competition is something consumers will object to and will confound any attempt to reduce imports.

One answer is for enterprises in developed countries to move further up market, though the actual scope for this can be exaggerated. The Swiss have set a good example with their precision instruments and watches. Indeed they have been so successful that they are one of the few industrialised countries to enjoy a favourable trade balance with Japan, even though they now face competition from Japanese electronic watches. Sections of our textile industry (particularly woollen and worsted fabrics) have achieved a favourable trade balance through high quality specialisation and provide us with substantial exports. In addition, we must expect the present trends towards more employment in the service sector to continue. This is not necessarily a bad thing.

Adjustment is necessary; but it must be both encouraged and tempered by Government action to provide a healthy environment for change. The principal industrial policies to this end are: financial assistance to encourage and accelerate new investment; fiscal investment incentives, measures to promote the mobility of labour, and retraining schemes. Throughout, the Government's aim is to promote commercially viable industry rather than necessarily to preserve existing enterprises. Here education, as well as enlightened planning by central and local authorities, has a vital part to play.

There are circumstances in which we already do, and may in the future also have to, restrict access to our own markets rather than hold unflinchingly to a doctrinaire policy on free trade. In recent years we have been faced increasingly often with the phenomenon of a rising flood of imports, often from the new super-competitive developing countries, threatening to disrupt our industry; this has happened in textiles, electronic consumer goods and footwear, and to some extent even in steel. In such circumstances, pressure for protection to save jobs can rapidly mount up. Yet if we yield unthinkingly to these demands we will in turn put at risk our access to developing country markets (which at present take no less than a quarter of our exports) and damage our development aid programme. Smooth adjustment is accordingly essential, and we must have the political will to tackle this rather than take a series of crisis measures.

Where the fast growth of imports from developing countries causes serious damage to our home industries, we are allowed to take safeguard measures under the rules of the GATT. The GATT Multifibre Arrangement is an example of what may be required. By the early 1970s the growth of textile imports from developing countries was so rapid that the whole industry in the developed world was being disrupted. International action had to be taken to regulate this trade. The original MFA therefore provided for quotas to be increased by at least 6 per cent per annum. For the majority of products, there was no restriction. But because of the recession there was virtually no growth in demand in the mid-1970s. As 6 per cent proved to be too fast in certain sensitive areas, in late 1977 the European Community negotiated bilateral agreements with some thirty supplying countries as an essential part of the renewal of the MFA, under which growth in sensitive sectors is still more restricted.

This is not outright, selfish protectionism. No one can say that the European Community has not adjusted; more than 500,000 jobs in the industry have been lost in the last few years. Growth, even if slow, is still provided for. And the European Community was able to reach agreement with the developing countries.

Moreover, the European Community differentiated between its suppliers, depending on how rich or poor they were. Hong Kong, Korea and Taiwan, all relatively rich, so-called 'super-competitive' suppliers, were restricted more than the poor countries such as India, Bangladesh and Sri Lanka, and the arrangements allow opportunities for new suppliers from developing countries to enter the market. Yet we cannot ignore the fact that our actions have worked against the poor developing countries, and in some instances gone against our own aid and development strategy to promote these very industries.

That is why, in any international situation, where protection is required to preserve jobs and to allow time for a smooth adjustment process, it should take account of development needs. In this way the harmful effects can at least be minimised. Far more important, however, is to anticipate and forestall the need for such action.

As far as resource transfers are concerned, although in current circumstances world economic management requires that some countries should sustain deficits sufficient to match the surpluses engendered by OPEC, rich countries in surplus could often dramatically increase their aid budgets. Not all developed countries have yet accepted the 0·7 per cent target for official assistance in principle. Those who have need to set their minds to putting it into practice within a reasonably short time. The problem worldwide is to give work to unemployed and under-employed labour and build up skills, so as to be more successful in meeting human desires, and particularly the basic needs of the most disadvantaged millions. Japan currently has an aid budget of 0·21 per cent of GNP. They plan to double this over five years. There are good reasons for their doubling it this coming financial year and then increasing it steadily. A massive increase of Japanese aid to the Third World is possible and desirable; by meeting the 0·7 per cent GNP target, the Japanese could inject as much as an additional $4 billion into the world economy. This is another example where the needs of the world economy for stimulus would be assisted by a policy aimed at developing countries, and vice versa.

In 1977 the British Government rightly decided that overseas aid should be increased; it became the fastest rising programme, with a substantial increase in the autumn and a steady 6 per cent increase in real terms from January 1978 onwards, so we are moving towards the 0·7 per cent aid target. Increased aid flows, in generating growth and purchasing power, help to build up markets in the developing world and hence to some extent to boost employment in major exporting nations such as ourselves. As a Government we do not tap sufficiently the altruistic impulse which exists in the community at large. Effective aid is not simply a matter of increased Government spending. The voluntary agencies have a vital role to play. Their flexibility and inventiveness can be invaluable where large bureaucratic machines appear insufficiently responsive to particular needs. We can continue to encourage people to contribute to the voluntary agencies by means of tax incentives, such as covenants. In some countries the annual tax return gives an opportunity for the citizen to give a percentage of income for a particular cause. As we move over to computerised tax returns it is not impossible to conceive an entry for overseas aid, and this need not mean that the voluntary agencies would find their resources drying up.

Other countries could do much more too. As far as the Soviet

Union and Eastern Europe are concerned, while they give a great deal of military aid there is very little real transfer of resources. While the United States's budget for military aid is about 24 per cent of the total aid budget, the equivalent in the Soviet aid budget is between 60 per cent and 70 per cent, and the remainder—including aid to communist developing countries—represents less than 0·1 per cent of Soviet GNP. Indeed, the value of Soviet aid to developing countries has declined since 1973–4, and debt service payments to the Soviet Union now exceed new disbursements to the least developed countries. While a few communist countries such as Cuba, Vietnam and Mongolia benefit from Soviet aid, the net effect of present Soviet aid policies is that of a resource transfer from the non-communist developing world to the Soviet Union. Soviet rhetoric—that because it was not a colonial power it has no obligation to assist in the development of Third World countries—is beginning to wear thin.

It will not be enough simply to increase our aid. We must also keep world attention focused on the financing of balance of payments deficits. Greater quantities of finance must be made available, sometimes on concessional terms. This in turn means increasing the lending capacity of the international financial institutions, in particular the IMF and the IBRD. It means more or larger loan facilities for developing countries. The US Congress here has a major responsibility to give the US administration the legislative authority it needs. It means increased co-operation between OPEC and its Special Fund and the OECD and its aid-giving offshoots.

In addition, we need to ensure as far as possible that our aid to developing countries reaches down to help those who most need it. If taxpayers in the developed world do not see aid money being spent in a way which helps alleviate poverty, then their resistance to giving more aid will increase. As in other areas of human rights policy, we must not delude ourselves that our views can have a dramatic effect. We cannot dictate; we can persuade and in extreme cases where there is abuse we can cut off aid which specifically buttresses such a Government. We must avoid reducing humanitarian aid and, while still trying to influence Governments, ensure that the individual within a country does not suffer. We cannot however use our views on aid or our views on human rights as a lever for us to determine the internal policies of other countries. But we can and should be vigilant in upholding the principles for which aid is given. The effect of our aid policies should be carefully monitored to see that the money over a period is not used to buttress social structures of manifest inequality even in poor countries.

While making it clear that our aim is to help both the poorest countries and the poorest in the poor countries, we need, then, to be careful to concentrate on achievable reforms and ignore the demands of the revolutionaries who oppose reforms merely because they want to bring forward the revolution. Under the Basic Needs Strategy we aim at the elimination of hunger and malnutrition, and the provision of food, clothing, shelter, water, health and education for the population of the world at an agreed minimum level by the year 2000. That is a realisable objective which could be achieved by careful monitoring and concentrated aid policies, working within the context of a world economy which would allow steady economic growth in developing countries. At the same time we must bear in mind that the Basic Needs Strategy must not be applied inflexibly. Developing countries will have differing views and standards. As the ILO *Declaration of Principles and Programme of Action* stated:

It is important to recognise that the concept of basic needs is a country-specific and dynamic concept. The concept of basic needs should be placed within a context of a nation's overall economic and social development. In no circumstances should it be taken to mean merely the minimum necessary for subsistence; it should be placed within a context of national independence, the dignity of the individual and peoples and their freedom to chart their destiny without hindrance.

But, as the European Community showed over Uganda, this is not a licence for a General Amin to do what he wishes. This is why Britain is adamant that the Lomé Convention, when renegotiated, must give some reserve powers to donor countries, and why there is the current debate in the IMF over human rights and the attitude of donor countries.

With these objectives the basic needs aid policy has common sense and justice on its side, and is indeed ambitious. Yet even this policy would be most unlikely to eliminate, even in the short term, the gap between rich and poor in the world. The poor would certainly become less poor, but a gap, a yawning gap, would remain. We need wider objectives which must include fairer distribution of scarce economic resources, wealth creation, employment creation and greater economic self-sufficiency.

If, for example, India were to succeed in increasing its per capita gross domestic product at an average rate of 6 per cent per year—and this would involve matching the recent performance of some of the fastest growing economies of the world —then (on the UN estimate of the present real per capita gap) it would take about fifty years for India to catch up with the *present* US level, by which time the United States will have moved on. Again this is not a prediction, but rather an illustration of the nature of the gap we cannot easily close. Bangladesh (or Ethiopia) may have been at about 75 per cent of the Indian level—hence less than 9 per cent of the UK level—in 1970. If these countries only managed an increase of 2 per cent per head between 1970 and 1990, they would reach about 13 per cent of the *present* UK level by 1990. Absolute living standards would have improved, but relative poverty would still be with us.

One key field where developed and developing countries could co-operate better is mineral exploitation. With our own North Sea oil in mind we can sympathise with the desire for 'permanent sovereignty over natural resources' expressed by the developing countries, particularly when those natural resources are potentially or actually their sole source of wealth. But we have not found a way of reconciling this principle with the need for investment. As a result the level of global economic activity is threatened through under-investment in minerals, and the tax and royalty receipts of the developing countries themselves are seriously affected. Mining is a long-term investment involving large sums of money. If the necessary investment is to be made then there must be confidence that there will be a fair division of the proceeds between those who have the mineral deposits and those who have the skills needed to work them.

Developed and developing countries alike have a responsibility to promote investment in new sources of energy and its conservation. It is, for example, in our interest to encourage developing countries to diversify their sources of energy. If there is an energy shortage in the 1990s, this will have dire consequences for all of us; and it is only too likely unless action is taken *now*. Investment lead times are long. The experts predict that energy prices will in any case rise in the 1980s and 1990s. Unless alternative sources of energy can be developed, the growing world demand for energy will continue to focus on oil. The resulting shortage could lead to big jumps in the price of oil – and we all know what that means for the world economy. Since some of the most important oil producers, such as Saudi Arabia, will be unable to spend their money, they will accumulate still larger financial surpluses. This will strain the world payments systems, augment deficits, and precipitate defaults as well as constraining world economic development. So developed and developing countries have every incentive to work together to stimulate the necessary investment in good time.

We must agree on measures to tackle the problems of international commodity trade. In part this is a matter of acting to stabilise prices around the long-term market trend – an important objective, though exaggerated claims are sometimes made for the effect it will have. The kind of fluctuations in price which we have experienced in recent years are bad for both producers and consumers; for producers because a lack of stability threatens investment and a reliable source of foreign exchange earnings; for consumers because lack of stability threatens the availability of supplies at reasonable prices.

Great stability is desired by both developed and developing countries. They are now working together under the auspices of UNCTAD on what is called the Integrated Programme for Commodities, or IPC. This programme has two main elements. The first involves work on individual commodities of interest to developing countries (and equally to developed consumers), the aim being in suitable cases to negotiate new price stabilising agreements or other arrangements for joint action by the producers and consumers concerned. The other element is the Common Fund. The establishment of a carefully and properly designed Common Fund could facilitate the financing of buffer stocks for existing and future Commodity Agreements. The basic idea is that Commodity Agreements can co-operate to achieve economies which would not be available to individual agreements operating on their own. Because commodity price movements do not always occur in phase, it is possible for Commodity Agreements which do not at a given moment have their resources tied up in buffer stocks to help finance the stocking operations of Commodity Agreements which need to build up stocks.

The Common Fund negotiations are currently stalled. It is in the interests of both developed and developing countries that they should be resumed—and that they should make real progress when they do resume. A reconvened conference which got nowhere would be worse than useless. This means flexibility on both sides—including recognition by the developing countries that if some of the proposals which have been floated were to be accepted, the Fund could become a nightmare, making no economic sense and helping the better-off countries rather than the poorest.

It is not surprising or unreasonable that there are many differing concepts of how such a fund should operate and be financed. But there does exist a consensus that any scheme eventually decided upon must assist international commodity arrangements to stabilise commodity prices around the longer-term market trends. This would be of benefit to developed and developing countries alike. Given goodwill and a bit of give and take, a basis exists for the successful conclusion of negotiations over a Common Fund.

The European Community recognises that wide fluctuations in commodity prices and export earnings can make a mockery of development plans. But these are complex problems and the solutions to them cannot be rushed through in one go. An impatience with what is seen as a slow process is understandable, but all international negotiations take time. Yet we recognise that it is literally a matter of life or death for many people that effective remedies for chronic poverty and malnutrition should be found, and soon. We should not belittle the considerable measure of agreement that has already been achieved by international negotiations. For this the European Community can rightly take a major share of the credit.

The Lomé Convention grants preferential access to Community markets to what were originally forty-six and are now fifty-two developing countries. Indicative aid programmes have been drawn up for all the original forty-six countries and aid is starting to flow for both national and regional products. The STABEX scheme has helped to stabilise export earnings in several raw materials. The establishment of the Centre for Industrial Development should increasingly bring into force the industrial co-operation provisions of the Convention. The full scope of the Convention was reviewed at the Second Joint Council meeting in Fiji in April 1977. The Community agreed to various improvements, including additions to the STABEX list which had been sought by the African, Caribbean and Pacific countries. It was generally agreed that the Convention was providing real benefits and was beginning to fulfil its promise as a model of co-operation between developed and developing countries, based on the principle of equal partnership.

In addition to a further programme of aid to a number of countries not associated with the Community under the Lomé Convention or other agreements, the Community's generalised scheme of preferences has been revised and improved in every year of its operation since its inception in 1971. It is now of particular benefit to the poorest developing countries. It provides for reduced duty, or duty-free, access for manufacturing and semi-manufacturing products. The Community has introduced its most recent improvement of the scheme in the face of economic recession, when many Community industries find themselves in difficulty and certain sectors are acutely vulnerable to low-cost imports from developing countries.

The Community's incentive has been part of a general effort by the industrialised world to remedy the imbalance between the richest and poorest nations. For example, agreement has recently been reached on replenishing the International Development Agency to the tune of more than $7 billion. The

IMF agreed at the end of 1975 on a liberalisation of the compensatory financing facility which resulted in a dramatic increase in drawings by commodity exporters. The IMF interim committee agreed at the beginning of last year to increase credit tranches by 45 per cent, pending the entry into force later this year of new members' quotas on average almost a third higher than existing quotas. This IMF committee is considering the possibility of greater access to the Fund's resources. Agreement was reached at the Kingston meeting of the IMF in January 1976 on gold sales over a period of four years, part of the proceeds of which goes into a trust fund for assistance to developing countries with balance of payments problems.

These are only some of the measures which the industrialised world has taken to assist the economic development of the poorer countries. In addition, within the framework of the Multilateral Trade Negotiations, a study is being undertaken of ways of improving the international framework for world trade with particular emphasis on trade between developed and developing countries.

It is a record of solid achievements. We have no grounds for complacency but neither have we grounds for despair or defeatism. It is a measure of the size of the problem that so much remains to be done. The European Community has always had a depressing tendency to denigrate its own achievements, often because it fixes its sights on unrealistic targets and then feels a sense of let-down. We must continue to offer the people of the poorer countries the prospect of lives no longer dominated by want and insufficiency. In doing so, we must ensure that we improve rather than damage the functioning of the world economic and trading system. This must be the standard by which we judge the validity and realism of the various issues which have arisen in the dialogue and of the solutions which have so far been proposed for them. This applies to debt relief, the export earning of producer countries and other issues.

Some of the ideas which have been discussed are frankly totally unrealistic and cannot be supported by politicians prepared to show vision and to give a lead to their domestic public opinion. It is simply not feasible to meet immediately all the demands of the developing world. Yet this practical political reality should not diminish the force of our commitment to deal co-operatively with the serious and urgent problems of developing countries. Resources are finite: and Governments which are democratically elected, and depend on popular support for their continuance in office, have to recognise the political constraints within which they work. This does not mean that the industrialised democracies are entitled to use their present economic difficulties as an excuse for abdicating the kind of political and economic leadership which the rest of the world rightly expects of them. On the contrary, our aim must be to establish a realistic basis on which to discuss with developing countries how resources can best be made to grow and how they should be deployed.

With perseverance and confidence in ourselves we should be able — meeting together with the rest of the world community — to take rational steps towards a peaceful evolution of the world economy. The aims — world economic recovery, adjustment, better aid policies, better investment policies and raw material price stabilisation — will no doubt be criticised as too limited, but they are achievable. Success will not be easy: but failure would be intolerable. The prize will not be heaven on earth, but a decent and tolerable world economic order for which our children, and perhaps our children's children, will be able to thank us, and which will enable us to share this planet, in peace and with a good conscience, with the other two-thirds of mankind at present in poverty.

Now that the worst of the economic crisis for Britain appears to have passed, we can take a more confident view of our ability to help correct the imbalance in the world economy. Within the European Community our record is mixed; we are better than most in concentrating on the poorest countries, about average in using multilateral agencies, but as to untying aid we are near the bottom of the list. Just as North Sea oil gives us the opportunity of investing in our industrial life-blood at home instead of frittering it away on ourselves, so we must use some of that bonus to invest more generously in a new world economic order.

9

World Peace

Our world, riven though it is by poverty and by social and economic injustice, devotes 6 per cent of what it produces to military expenditure. We manage collectively to spend $1 billion a day on armaments, a figure which is equivalent to the combined incomes of almost half the world's population who live in the thirty-six poorest countries. This is double the world's expenditure on health and larger than its expenditure on education. In two days the world spends on defence the equivalent of a year's budget for the UN and its specialised agencies: and in three hours the equivalent of a year's budget for UN peace-keeping.

Human and industrial resources too are absorbed into the military field on a vast scale. Fifty-seven million people are estimated to be employed as members of armed forces or in jobs related to military activity. Half a million scientists and engineers are engaged in military research and development which, according to some estimates, accounts for 40 per cent of the world's research and development in all fields.

These are striking figures. We ought, as a world community, to determine to reduce the drain on our scarce resources which this level of military expenditure involves. For socialist and social democratic parties it is a major challenge. Those of us who seek in our own countries to create a society based on democratic socialist ideals and on a more equitable distribution of wealth and resources cannot fail to be aware of the economic burdens which the maintenance of our military establishments imposes. As internationalists we must recognise that it will be difficult to bring about a fairer international distribution of wealth and an improvement in the economic circumstances of the countries of the developing world as long as they are forced to follow, as inevitably they will be, the path of the industrialised nations in devoting a significant proportion of their national income to building up their military strength.

But the problem is not just one of economic management or resource allocation. It has a crucial moral and political dimension as well. So long as the world remains as heavily armed as it now is, wars will continue. Even relatively small-scale and local wars can cause a vast amount of human suffering and destruction—as we have seen ever since 1947 in the Middle East, in Vietnam and as we are increasingly seeing in Africa. Moreover, so long as the present level of military confrontation, both nuclear and conventional, between East and West is allowed to remain, the risks of a world war on a scale eclipsing anything that has ever gone before can never be wholly discounted.

The avoidance of war and the search for a system of international security which will cause nations no longer to rely on the use or the threat of the use of military force as an instrument of their international policies must therefore be for all of us an overriding aim. Disarmament can contribute to this in two ways. First, and most directly, it can reduce the material means available with which wars can be fought. Secondly, and perhaps more importantly, it can help create a climate of trust and confidence in which states will be less disposed to look to military power as a means of preserving their own security.

Three-quarters of the world's military expenditure is accounted for by the developed world, and nearly two-thirds by the United States and the Soviet Union. Britain, with 3·3 per cent of world GNP, accounts for 2·7 per cent of military expenditure. The developing countries are right to insist that the northern hemisphere should show the lead in disarmament. They are right in this situation of overkill and underdevelopment to call for a diversion of resources from military to economically and socially productive expenditure to the benefit of all peoples. They are aware that the military expenditure of the OECD states is eleven times greater than the aid they provide to the developing world; and for the COMECON states the ratio of military expenditure to aid is 400:1.

In the 1950s and 1960s serious attempts were made to deal with the whole disarmament problem in one comprehensive treaty on general and complete disarmament. This was too ambitious, especially given the sharp tension which then existed between East and West. These efforts failed not just because of lack of confidence but because insufficient attention was given to how people and states actually behave, and too much attention to how they ought to behave. Now we try to progress by achieving wherever possible specific measures valuable in themselves, and hope to create the confidence needed for further, more ambitious treaties. This approach is, however, firmly bureaucratised and institutionalised. Progress depends on consensus—the military have an inbuilt caution expressed in the doctrine that 'everything must be balanced and simultaneous'—so movement is very slow. Step-by-step changes with a political impetus offer a much greater chance of progress, and the risks of this have to be offset against the risks of continuing as we do at present. The problem is that each country or group of countries is hesitant to make the first move. We are in danger of being immobilised by the wish to march in step towards disarmament and no one is prepared to be the first to break ranks.

A few important agreements have been reached but in the main politicians claim more progress than is actually justified. The Partial Test Ban Treaty in 1963 was a real advance, greatly reducing the danger to mankind from radioactive fallout from atmospheric tests. The Non-Proliferation Treaty of 1968 is not a perfect instrument, but over a hundred states have adhered and the Treaty has undoubtedly reduced the risks of weapons proliferation. The Biological Weapons Convention of 1972, though unverified, was a measure of genuine disarmament, requiring the destruction of all stocks of a particularly horrible type of weapon. The US-Soviet Anti-Ballistic Missile Treaty of 1972 was a major success, for it ruled out the nation-wide deployment of a type of defence which could have increased the waste of resources and destabilised deterrence between the superpowers. The SALT I Interim Agreement on Strategic Offensive Weapons was the start of what could offer the possibility of controlling the strategic nuclear arms race.

The policy of concentrating on specific measures has, therefore, produced some results but they are meagre and many people are rightly impatient for speedier progress. East-West relations are far better today, and East-West contacts in many fields immeasurably more intensive than they were when, in 1963, we resumed the search for disarmament through a series of specific treaties. The improvement in the climate has been brought about in part by the achievement of the arms control treaties. And the existence of that climate in turn justifies our being now more ambitious in arms control. We should recognise that the only way we can advance is by specific agreements. But we should combine the agreements and other measures we are seeking into a co-ordinated, coherent, single plan. The first such plan might cover a period of five years. It should be followed by another for the next period after that. Each plan would then be a map of part of the road towards the Utopian objective of general and complete disarmament.

The UN Special Session on Disarmament in the summer of 1978 was useful in that it involved many Heads of Government and attracted the attention of the media. It should encourage arms control research in the universities and institutes, and enhance the role of the United Nations in disarmament. It will probably also result in reform of the international machinery concerned with negotiation and discussion of this crucial subject.

Progress over disarmament will require willingness by each group of states to understand the problems of the other groups. The developed states cannot expect the developing ones suddenly to stop importing arms. And the non-aligned cannot expect—nor in their own interests should they desire—the wholesale and hasty dismantling of the system of deterrence in the northern hemisphere. But each can expect from the other that a serious start will be made on these issues in the years following the Special Session, so that a second Programme of Action can call for more radical measures.

In the Special Session the non-aligned countries stressed the primacy of nuclear disarmament. They were right to do so. Nuclear weapons have the potential to cause a disaster many times greater than mankind has ever known. No one, in seeing the way in which nuclear weapons technology has developed, could surely wish otherwise than that the atom bomb and its successor systems had never been invented. That the technology for making such weapons exists we can do nothing about. But we must try to ensure that the technology is not developed further and that the existing stocks of such weapons are reduced and eventually eliminated. Since reliance on nuclear weapons is central to the defence policies of the most powerful nations of the world and since it cannot be denied that the system of mutual deterrence has preserved a degree of security over the last thirty years or so, it would be foolish to try to dismantle this system of deterrence in an imbalanced or ill-considered way. None the less, we should not regard the present pattern of nuclear confrontation between East and West as something to be lived with for all time. The security which it affords us is at best a fragile one. And we cannot expect to achieve progress either globally or regionally in the conventional arms field unless we are prepared to work for serious measures of nuclear disarmament.

The central negotiation for nuclear arms control is the series of Strategic Arms Limitation Talks (SALT). They are crucial for the development of East-West relations generally and for the future of detente. The SALT process, which began in Helsinki in 1969, is in itself probably the most significant international event since the end of the Second World War. The SALT I agreements show that it is possible for the US and the Soviet Union to reach understandings about controlling the strategic nuclear arms race. But these agreements were just a beginning. The negotiations for a second SALT agreement have been long and difficult. But we should not forget that this is not only one of the most important negotiations in the history of arms control, it is also probably the most complex. The fact that the discussions have been kept going in a reasonably constructive and businesslike fashion is itself encouraging.

The SALT I interim agreement merely set limits beyond which neither the US nor the Soviet Union could increase their strategic forces without dismantling older systems. It was in fact a freeze in numbers. The SALT II agreement, however, will mean an actual reduction in numbers albeit on a modest scale, coupled with some qualitative restraints to slow down the momentum of competitive development of strategic nuclear systems. SALT II will thus be a landmark in curbing vertical proliferation, that is, the increase of weapons among nuclear weapon states. It should be accorded an unreserved welcome and should be recognised as a major achievement by the two superpowers in reducing, for the first time, by agreement their nuclear arsenals in a way which jeopardises neither their own security nor that of their allies.

The negotiation of reductions in the strategic forces of the US and the Soviet Union should become a continuous process. Even after the SALT II agreement, the two superpowers will retain a massive degree of overkill in their strategic armouries, and drastic further reductions in their ballistic missile stockpiles would still leave each side able to inflict an assured degree of destruction on the other. President Carter's reference in 1977 to the possibility of a 50 per cent reduction in strategic arms by the US and the Soviet Union was a recognition of this. The US and Soviet Union should be encouraged to think in terms of a reduction of this kind for any SALT III agreement. It will not be easy to get the Soviet leadership, particularly the Soviet military leadership, to think in as radical and as imaginative terms as this. They must be persuaded that reductions of this kind would not prejudice their own security and would be a major contribution to world peace, to the achievement of which they have so often purported to commit themselves.

The 1978 decision by President Carter to postpone production of the enhanced radiation warhead or neutron bomb was, in the circumstances, absolutely right and thoroughly praiseworthy. Whatever the military attractions of a weapon of this kind, and although it could not unfairly be represented as a relatively minor piece of technological innovation in the nuclear weapons field, there were obvious political dangers in introducing it into Europe at that time. So long as there remains a chance that withholding its deployment may contribute to a more productive arms control climate, then the balance of advantage remains in favour of *not* introducing it. It is right that the leaders of the two superpowers should think very carefully before introducing qualitative or quantitative changes to their nuclear forces. President Carter has shown considerable courage on the B1 bomber decision and over the neutron bomb. So far, the Soviet leadership has not shown this sort of political will. They must now realise that the onus is on them to show a commensurate restraint over those elements of their own forces, both nuclear and conventional, which cause apprehension in the minds of other countries.

The neutron bomb was not a weapons system which came into the orbit of the SALT talks. Nor are some of the other nuclear weapons, for example the new Soviet SS20 missile, which arouse public concern. Sooner or later weapons of this kind will need to be brought within the framework of arms control discussions. European security will not be enhanced if, at a time when the strategic nuclear balance is being regulated through SALT and when efforts are being made to achieve a conventional arms control regime in Europe through MBFR, theatre range nuclear weapons are allowed to proliferate without restraint. The difficulties involved are formidable, because of the different numbers and types of the systems concerned and the range of countries directly or indirectly affected. But in some forum discussion will have to take place.

A comprehensive test ban covering all nuclear explosions would be a major obstacle to the development of new warheads by nuclear weapon states, and thus to vertical proliferation. It would also be a considerable contribution to the cause of curbing horizontal proliferation, the spread of nuclear weapon technology to non-nuclear weapon states.

In this general field of horizontal proliferation, the objective must be to promote an international consensus on how to provide access to the peaceful uses of nuclear energy while minimising the risk of weapons proliferation.

The issues of nuclear non-proliferation are complex. But the central problem can be reduced to brutally simple terms. The world is increasingly forced to look to nuclear power as a means of sustaining life, in the full knowledge that nuclear power, if misused, adds to the danger of destroying life once and for all. The dilemma is unprecedented in human history. None of us—nuclear and non-nuclear states alike—has yet fully come to terms with its implications. The ill-wind of the Indian nuclear explosion of 1974 had one immediately beneficial effect: it shook the complacency of many countries, Britain included. We have little time left in which to develop an international strategy — the only kind of strategy which will work — to contain the dangers of nuclear weapons proliferation.

Nuclear non-proliferation is an area in which Britain has an influential voice. We are one of only five nuclear weapon states; we are one of the three depositary powers of the Non-Proliferation Treaty; we built the first commercial nuclear power reactor to go on stream more than twenty years ago; we are among the leaders in developing new technology in commercial enrichment, reprocessing and fast reactors; and we are Chairman and hosts of the Nuclear Suppliers Group. Britain cannot play a major role in every area of international political and diplomatic activity; but in nuclear matters this country has the standing, and the duty, to make a distinctive contribution.

We cannot claim to have cut-and-dried answers to what is one of the gravest problems facing the international community. The challenge is, however, such that we are all duty-bound to be constantly receptive to new thinking from whatever quarter. We should not be ashamed to admit that, with a greater knowledge and awareness, we must progressively tighten up our procedures and sometimes change past policies.

Some argue that there are no physical controls at the disposal of suppliers, whether or not they possess nuclear weapons, which can guarantee absolutely that access to fissile material and the capability to make a bomb will not spread. This is true; but in very few areas of life can we be certain of an absolute guarantee. To argue from this that we should not make the maximum effort to prevent the spread of nuclear weapons, that we should relax the stringency of the safeguards we are seeking, is an argument not only of despair, but of folly. International action has so far been slow, ineffective and insufficient. There have been men of vision, there have been important achievements, but judged overall politicians have allowed the urgency and dangers to be swamped by commercial interest and bureaucratic indifference.

About a dozen countries have now the basic knowledge and access to fissile materials required to produce nuclear explosive devices. It has been estimated that by 1987 a further twenty states could be in a similar position, if they took the decision now. This is a frightening prospect. Even without a commercial nuclear power programme, any relatively industrialised state, if it were determined to produce the plutonium for a bomb, could build a reactor and a small reprocessing plant.

The blunt truth is that, if the international community is to eliminate proliferation, it must remove the incentive to acquire nuclear weapons and that means pursuing detente and serious, balanced measures of disarmament to the full. Some of those countries which could soon become nuclear weapon states are to be found in areas of regional instability and insecurity, either actual or potential. There is a direct link between removing the incentive to acquire nuclear weapons and the creation of conditions of stability and security; the reverse of the coin is a recipe for nuclear conflict. The quantitative threat of proliferating nuclear weapons can only be contained by a qualitative improvement in the management of international relations.

It is therefore essential to foster an international climate hostile to the proliferation of nuclear weapons. The first steps were taken ten years ago with the Non-Proliferation Treaty. The Treaty remains the centrepiece of non-proliferation strategy. It reflects the special responsibilities of the nuclear weapon states. Regrettably only three of them have ratified the Treaty. But France has made it clear that she will act as if she were a party; and I do not believe that China wishes to encourage proliferation. Thirty or so non-nuclear weapon states have also failed to adhere, among whom several have growing nuclear industries.

We must encourage more states to adhere to the Non-Proliferation Treaty. Britain, together with the United States and the Soviet Union, the other co-depositary powers, has had considerable success in bringing states under the Treaty's umbrella: in the last two years, twenty-one states, some of them very important, have adhered. Altogether there are 104 states party to the Non-Proliferation Treaty including all but one member state of the European Community. It is a significant asset that this is an area in which East and West work closely together, reflecting their common interest in avoiding nuclear war. The irony is that the two sides are co-operating closely to confine a danger which in large part springs from their mutual suspicion and competition.

The commitment in the Non-Proliferation Treaty to curb the spread of nuclear weapons is accompanied by the equally important commitment under Article 4 to promote the further development of nuclear energy for peaceful purposes. The central dilemma is how best to reconcile these two objectives.

An effective non-proliferation strategy must go hand in hand with a viable energy strategy. This in turn means that we have to take interlocking decisions on different sources of energy — their rates of conservation, exploitation, diversification — and relate these decisions to the even more fundamental issue of the kind of world we want to live in: what should be its primary means of transport, its source of heat and light; what balance should be struck between the need for energy and the need to protect the environment. There are also important civil liberty issues about what level of physical security is tolerable in peacetime for civil installations. At the present moment, although at last we have started openly to debate the issues, in none of the industrialised democracies have we arrived at a national consensus on how they should be resolved.

The back-cloth against which a non-proliferation strategy has to be urgently hammered out is one of a prospective shortage of energy, reinforced by the economic and structural consequences flowing from ever-increasing prices. Present forecasts show world demand for oil far exceeding supply by the mid-1980s. Some predict a world energy crisis before the end of the century. Prediction is a hazardous business but there is no question of the need to increase nuclear energy to help meet the world's energy requirements. The plain truth is that some countries have no alternative to nuclear power and even those with plentiful oil and coal know these cannot continue indefinitely.

This said, the objective of the 'technical' component in non-proliferation strategy must still be to place the most stringent controls on access to the technology and fissile materials necessary to produce atomic weapons. The present position is that IAEA safeguards apply to all the civil nuclear activities of the non-weapon states who are parties to the Non-Proliferation

Treaty; in addition Britain and the United States, although nuclear weapon states, have voluntarily accepted IAEA safeguards on those parts of their nuclear industry which supply their civil nuclear programmes. The Nuclear Suppliers Group has established guidelines designed to remove safeguards and controls from the area of commercial competition.

It is a measure of the size of the problem that, despite these efforts, the present situation is unsatisfactory and unacceptable. We must constantly strive to make the international safeguards system as watertight as possible. New thinking is needed if we are to achieve our dual purpose of promoting non-proliferation and building up mutual confidence between nuclear and non-nuclear powers. The UK has advocated the general application of full fuel cycle safeguards and a model agreement has been drawn up by the IAEA, at Britain's instigation, to enable nations who are not party to the Non-Proliferation Treaty to accept these safeguards. We welcome the American Government's decision in 1977 to endorse this. It is a significant change in their position and we hope that others will follow their example.

President Carter in 1977 put forward wide-ranging and complex proposals which go far further than anything proposed hitherto. Their purpose is to remove the incentive for more countries to acquire their own enrichment and reprocessing capability, which could be used for military purposes; to offer them instead assured supplies of enriched fuel to meet all their power needs; and so to seek their acceptance of what is coming to be called the 'throw-away' fuel cycle, which would dispense with commercial reprocessing and plutonium-based fuel cycles altogether. These proposals merit the most detailed and careful evaluation before we reach any final conclusions on the best means of achieving non-proliferation objectives and at the same time satisfying the energy requirements of countries other than the United States. This international fuel cycle evaluation started in 1978 and is unlikely to be completed before 1980. In Britain we will approach it seriously, with an open mind and a firm commitment to non-proliferation; but it is too early to pass definitive judgments and there are a number of questions which we shall have to take into account.

The first is whether there will be sufficient uranium available to meet the world's energy demands without plutonium. Are uranium reserves in non-communist countries sufficient to meet the demands of reactors planned for construction by the mid-1990s? If so, for how much longer? The Ford Mitre Study thought that at projected rates of demand there would be no difficulty about fulfilling requirements for uranium up to the turn of the century. Other authorities take a different view. Either way, what happens after the turn of the century? Will uranium ore follow the same general history as most other minerals? That is, with foreseeable advances in technology and changed economic conditions, will it be possible to exploit ores and reserves of progressively lower grade and lesser accessibility? Once upon a time no one would have touched copper below a yield of 20 per cent. Today $\frac{1}{2}$ per cent copper is economic in some parts of the world. In the latter half of the nineteenth century no one would have touched the low-grade iron ore which we now mine in the UK. How much difference will higher prices (and what prices?) make to the availability of uranium and the economies of nuclear power generation? The answers to these questions will greatly affect the policy conclusions we draw.

Assuming the existence of sufficient uranium worldwide, there is still anxiety as to whether it would be safe for any country to depend on supplies from others. The United States and Canada alone among Western countries are in a position to meet their needs into the next century from their own resources. To rely heavily on uranium imports raises serious questions. It can be argued that reprocessing and the eventual use of fast breeder reactors would lessen, or eliminate, dependence on possibly uncertain uranium supplies for those countries with none of their own. We need to ask ourselves whether there is a qualitative difference between dependence in the case of uranium and dependence in the case of food, let alone oil. We need also to ask ourselves whether, if there are countries who cannot do without reprocessing, they will not be driven to develop their own facilities from existing technology, should countries like Britain and France withdraw the reprocessing services they now offer to others. The examples of Brazil and Pakistan have shown that the incentive to have reprocessing facilities exists.

There are strong arguments for urging, on non-proliferation grounds, that reprocessing, if it is to take place, should do so in as few countries as possible.

The same considerations apply to enriching uranium. Uranium has to be treated, and slightly enriched, before it is usable as fuel for most civil nuclear power stations. We must remember — and we must not allow it to be overlooked in the present discussions — that a nuclear bomb can be made from highly enriched uranium as easily, if not more easily, than from plutonium.

Assuming we can find satisfactory answers to these problems, there are still important political and technical questions about the throw-away cycle and whether it contributes to non-proliferation objectives as much as is claimed. What kind of system, for example, should be devised for storing spent fuel, bearing in mind that it would still contain large quantities of plutonium, which could be separated at any time, and which would in logic require the same degree of international controls as apply to reprocessing? Can a satisfactory disposal route be identified for spent fuel elements and, if not, can they be stored indefinitely from a technical point of view? Our own Magnox fuel elements, for example, must be reprocessed. Would the indefinite storage of unreprocessed spent fuel elements be acceptable environmentally? Densely populated countries in Europe and Japan will inevitably be concerned about the safety problems. What are the economic and energy implications of the American proposals? Will a throw-away cycle be more expensive, counting storage and fuel costs? If an alternative to the throw-away cycle can be shown to be equally effective on non-proliferation grounds and cheaper in terms of energy cost and consumption, it would clearly be preferable. So we cannot make these judgments without any economic assessment. We should not shrink from paying higher costs if this would achieve greater safety and reduce the risks of proliferation. Non-proliferation objectives must not be sacrificed to the application of narrowly based cost-effective criteria. In sum, what fuel cycle would most effectively contribute to non-proliferation objectives while taking into account environmental and energy supply considerations? This is the central issue.

The answers will hopefully come about through international agreement based on the recognition that all countries, whatever their stage of development, have a legitimate requirement for timely assurances that their future energy needs, including nuclear, will be met; and that, without such assurances, general agreement on measures to control, in the name of non-proliferation, the use of nuclear energy for peaceful purposes will not be possible. The countries of the world have also an abiding interest in curtailing the threat to the human race posed by proliferation. These issues, and their reconciliation, can only be dealt with satisfactorily by a long-term process of continuous and open-ended negotiation.

It may be that a new awareness of these fundamental considerations will develop. If so, we are on a course which offers the possibility that nuclear energy will ultimately contribute to humanity's salvation, not to its destruction.

Another approach to this problem of horizontal proliferation is to seek to reduce the incentive to states to acquire nuclear weapons. It may be possible to give leading non-nuclear weapon states satisfactory assurances that nuclear weapons will not be used against them or deployed in their regions.

Nuclear arms control agreements and measures to prevent the proliferation of nuclear weapons, though important, are only part of the disarmament process. In global terms, the major arms build-up now taking place is in conventional weapons and this build-up needs to be the subject of international arms control agreements. We must try to halt, and if possible reverse, this trend. Negotiations in Vienna for European force reductions have virtually stagnated now for five years and a major political effort will be needed to move them forward out of the present impasse. Lately there have been some slightly more hopeful signs, in that the two sides in the talks have at last managed to agree on exchanging data on an acceptable basis and the West has tabled new proposals. But without common understanding on the figures for the forces of the two military alliances in Europe it will obviously be extremely difficult to find a way to achieve reductions which will be accepted as equitable by all the participants.

Difficult and complex though these talks are, agreement

would be a major prize which would add a new dimension to the whole detente process. It ought to be common ground between the participants that the eventual outcome should be a situation of military parity between the two sides in central Europe. Reductions which lead to parity, a principle which has already been accepted in SALT, cannot be regarded as prejudicial to either side's security. There is at present a disturbing military imbalance in central Europe which, although in a sense only local, none the less is a source of very considerable concern to the countries of the North Atlantic Alliance. It is legitimate for these countries to ask, without imputing any malign intentions to the Soviet Union and its allies, why it is that the Warsaw Pact needs to maintain a degree of military capability deployed forward in central Europe which so significantly outnumbers, in terms both of men and major types of equipment, the forces deployed on the other side. The MBFR talks offer an opportunity of establishing a balanced and equal relationship between the two military alliances at a reduced level of forces. There are no aspirations on the Western side to military superiority over the Warsaw Pact.

The international arms trade will only be controlled if two principles of vital importance are accepted. First, that no state shall be deprived by others of its right to self-defence under the UN Charter. And second, that suppliers and recipients must explore the problem together and co-operate in devising ways of tackling it. The problem is too controversial and — regrettably — insufficiently understood for immediate agreements. The Special Session has stimulated interest and the discussion instigated by President Carter among the major arms producers may produce some results, but there are national economic employment and foreign policy implications which will be extremely hard to resolve.

Budgetary limitation is another way to control the global arms race. One of the problems of disarmament is that there are important military activities which cannot be verifiably controlled in numerical terms. A good example is military research and development. The broad budgetary approach to arms control has the advantage — if Governments do not cheat — that it covers the whole of military expenditure, including those activities which cannot be tackled individually in a quantitative way. The other great advantage of acting upon military budgets directly is that limitations or reductions may be applied to the whole range of military activities, not just to specific sectors. Successfully applied, it could produce an actual transfer of resources from the military sector to peaceful purposes, and it is this central aim of transferring resources from armaments to development which will be the major theme of all disarmament discussion in the 1980s.

The difficulty with the budgetary approach is that it relies on Governments' revealing the true facts, and a common assessment is needed in order to compare one budget with another. Useful work on devising a standard method for reporting military expenditure has been done under the auspices of the UN Secretary General. This method should be used for reporting military spending on a worldwide basis, as a step towards balanced and verified reductions. Secretiveness breeds suspicion and is incompatible with the budgetary approach to disarmament. This course has often been advocated by the Warsaw Pact, but they as yet refuse to reveal details of their military budgets and adopt a much more restrictive information policy than the West.

We also need to know more about the relationship between disarmament and development. The new UN study of this subject sponsored by the Nordic countries should pay particular attention to the problems of conversion and redeployment of the resources released from military purposes to civilian use.

The United Nations does valuable work in collecting statistics in many important fields like agriculture and health, yet so far it has had little involvement over world security statistics. Collecting information has been left to independent bodies and the influence and prestige of the UN has not been used to disclose comprehensive data. The Disarmament Centre in the UN Secretariat has taken on a larger role in recent years. Some, however, still oppose the further extension of the Centre's work, resisting the UN Disarmament Yearbook's inclusion of statistics on armaments and military expenditure. Some nations wish to limit any internationalising of security issues. Yet we should consider it as natural to exchange information and expertise in the field of international security as we do in other areas. We need to understand more about each other's perceptions of security. We need to resist the tendency to think of security as a purely national matter. If we are to preserve the right of the individual to live in peace and security we must give disarmament a higher national and international priority than hitherto.

We must keep stressing the appalling magnitude of the problems of the arms race and the imperative need to achieve speedier progress. Complacency in this area of human activity can easily trigger our own destruction. The risks are real, the dangers ever-present.

Index